THE TRADITIONAL
AGA
BOOK OF
BREADS & CAKES

THE TRADITIONAL
AGA
BOOK OF
BREADS
& CAKES

Louise Walker

A.

Absolute Press

First published in 2003 by Absolute Press,
an imprint of Bloomsbury Publishing Plc

Bloomsbury Publishing Plc
50 Bedford Square, London WC1B 3DP
www.bloomsbury.com

Absolute Press
Scarborough House
29 James Street West
Bath BA1 2BT
England
Phone 44 (0) 1225 316013
Fax 44 (0) 1225 445836
E-mail office@absolutepress.co.uk
Website www.absolutepress.co.uk

Reprinted 2013

A catalogue record of this book is
available from the British Library

ISBN 9781899791743

Cover and text illustrations
by Caroline Nisbett

Printed and bound by CPI Group (UK) Ltd, Croydon, CR0 4YY

CONTENTS

GENERAL
INTRODUCTION

INTRODUCTION

Although breads and cakes are widely available in our shops and supermarkets it has become increasingly popular to bake your own at home. Not only can it be a very enjoyable and rewarding thing to do, the results are usually much better and a lot tastier.

Over the years, many people have asked me for advice on baking breads and cakes in their Agas. I'm always happy to tell them that breads, cakes and Agas go perfectly well together, after all, the Aga seems to be the best bread-making machine there is, and cakes baked in the Aga will come out beautifully moist.

You may, of course, have heard the myth, 'you can't bake a cake in an Aga'. This is simply not true. Whilst I'll concede that sometimes two-oven Aga owners need a trick or two up their sleeves to achieve a good, even bake, three- and four-oven Agas present no problems whatsoever. Just one of the reasons why so many Aga-baked cakes are sold at Women's Institute and Farmers' Markets each week!

For both the bread and cake sections I have included some general advice and tips, so if you are new to Aga baking then it's worth spending a few minutes reading these before you proceed. Making bread is not difficult; I will take you through the basic steps. If you have not made bread before, I suggest you start with a simple white or brown loaf and then make it again several times over. This should accustom you to handling the ingredients and getting a general feel for the yeast dough, and instruct you as to how your Aga works for baking. Making a Victoria Sandwich is as good an introduction to cakes as you can get – it is such a versatile cake because it can be filled, topped and flavoured in such a variety of ways. Try a few of these variations and then get your teeth into the recipes that follow.

CONVERSION CHART

This is the metric/imperial chart that I abide by. Do keep to either metric or imperial measures throughout the whole recipe. Mixing the two can lead to all kinds of problems. Eggs used in testing have been size 3. 'Tablespoon' and 'teaspoon' measures have been flat unless otherwise stated.

Ingredients	Conversion
1 oz	25g
2 oz	50g
3 oz	75g
4 oz	100g
5 oz	150g
6 oz	175g
7 oz	200g
8 oz	225g
9 oz	250g
10 oz	275g
11 oz	300g
12 oz	350g
13 oz	375g
14 oz	400g
15 oz	425g
16 oz (1 lb)	450g
2 lb	1kg
1 teaspoon	5ml
1 tablespoon	15ml
¼ pint	150ml
½ pint	300ml
¾ pint	450ml
1 pint	600ml
2 pints	1.2l
8-inch tin	20-cm tin

LOOKING AFTER YOUR AGA

Over the last few years Aga-Rayburn have brought out a few new items of cookware. I am lucky in that I can try these in the showrooms during cookery demonstrations before I buy. Utensils are expensive and so you need to know that you will get value for money. All the Aga Shops and dealer's shops should have a good range of equipment. All the items made for Aga have been tested and, if looked after, will last as long as your Aga. I have seen a set of saucepans bought with a new Aga 48 years ago and just one handle had come off in that time! Remember to dry everything well before putting away, but that is easy, wash and put straight back on the Aga to dry. Don't put aluminium trays and pans in the dishwasher, the salt will eat them!

A new Aga comes with:

A large and small roasting tin with a grill rack inside each. These tins fit on the runners.

A cold shelf (plain shelf) to vary the oven temperature. Keep out of the oven so that it can be effective when you need it. It is also a useful baking tray for making giant pizzas.

Oven shelves. These are always the subject of 'help me out' at new owner demonstrations. The shelves have an anti-tilt design which is easy to use when you know what you are doing. However if you get your shelf stuck ask your service engineer or go to an Aga Shop where you can probably practice on a cold Aga. Just remember, lift the shelf up before pulling out!

Although these are the basics that the Aga comes with, in my opinion there are three more essentials that I think new owners should buy:

An Aga kettle. What a waste of heat it is not to use a kettle on the Aga. Do remember to give it a rinse out at least once a day and keep it as scale-free as possible. Where I live, in Bath, we must have some of the hardest water in the country, keeping the spout of the kettle clean is a constant battle! If your kettle seems to take a long time to come to the boil give the hot plate a brush with the wire brush, just a few toast crumbs can stop the water boiling.

Gauntlets can take a little time to get used to but if you don't want burn marks up your arm they are an essential item. The Aga gauntlets can seem stiff and unwieldy when they are new but after a couple of washes they will soften up.

Bake-O-Glide is a great boon if you don't like washing up or cutting parchment to line cake tins. Bake-O-Glide is a re-usable non-stick liner that simply needs a wash in hot soapy water after each use and will mean that tins only need a quick wash rather than a soak and scrub. This magic liner can be bought in a roll or, even easier, from the Aga shops you can get it as a set for all the Aga tins.

Apart from those essentials I have mentioned one or two other pieces of equipment throughout this book:

Baking tray. Several years ago Aga brought out a baking tray similar to the roasting tin. At first I couldn't see the reason to have a shallow tin when the roasting tin worked so well. Now I have to eat my words. I have the large and small size and use them practically every day. Because they are shallow roast vegetables, for example, cook faster and better than in the roasting tin. These tins of course fit on the oven runners. In some recipes in this book I have stated a shelf position. If you have the Aga tins use that runner or put the shelf on the runner suggested and your own tin on that.

The wok and the ridged pan. Aga now make a heavy wok with a flat base to make contact with the hotplate. To have a successful stir-fry it is essential that the wok is hot before you start cooking. Place the empty wok on the boiling plate for at least ten minutes, yes, ten minutes! During Aga demonstrations I know that the wok is getting hot because the audience shows signs of concern, expecting the whole thing to explode! When the wok is hot start cooking quickly as the oil will burn if you haven't got the ingredients ready to go in straight away. Similarly, the ridged pan. Choose one with deep ridges that can be heated well. Cast iron is the best, but heavy. There is never any need to put oil in these pans, anyway the oil would disappear into the base of the pan and be of no use. If you want to 'grill' vegetables, however, then brush them with oil before putting them in the pan. Again, you need to heat the pan for a minimum of ten minutes, and you can do this on the floor of the roasting oven if the pan handle is ovenproof.

A timer. This is essential as food cooking in the Aga will not be smelt, unless of course if you go in the garden! Try and obey the timer. I have two problems with timers. Firstly if I am busy when the timer rings I think I will check the ovens in a minute, and often don't! Secondly the timer rings and I can't think of anything in the oven so don't check! We have our fair share of charcoal dishes.

COOKING WITH THE AGA

You will have more success with your Aga if you understand the reasoning behind strange instructions like 'cooking potatoes in the oven'. The Aga uses stored heat. The ovens cook well when they are heated to their optimum temperature, your engineer will explain this, and will cook with a lovely even heat. As soon as the hotplate lids are lifted there is going to be some heat loss. Obviously this is not significant if just boiling a kettle or making toast, but cooking a pan of potatoes ready to mash will lower the oven temperature. So, always think, can this be done in the oven? The other advantage here is that you don't have pans boiling dry and steam and smells filling the kitchen.

To help keep the heat even in the Aga the lids on the hotplates are insulated and fairly heavy. Keep these lids down when not using the hotplates. The outer part of the lid is either chrome, stainless steel or cast iron. These will in time scratch so look after them. To non-Aga owners the boiling plate lid is the perfect place to put the kettle! Use a protective Chef's Pad, folded tea towel or a trivet to protect the lids. I find that I don't use my hot plates very much. Boiling the kettle and making toast are the obvious examples. The boiling plate is also used to bring water to the boil, start vegetables or rice cooking, and of course wok cooking and making pancakes in a frying pan. The simmering plate is the place to make sauces, Welsh cakes and drop scones, toasted sandwiches and gravy.

Otherwise steaming, grilling and frying are usually done in the roasting oven. The ovens might look small from the outside but they are Tardis-like inside. The whole of the oven can be used as there is no single source of heat to spoil the food. It is not uncommon for the roasting oven to have an area where the food cooks marginally faster than the rest of the oven. All my gas Agas have been slightly hotter towards the back on the left-hand side of the roasting oven. This only causes a problem when doing large tray-bakes or trays of bread rolls, when turning the tray halfway through cooking usually solves that problem. All the ovens on an Aga, whether two or four are the same size.

I once had a gentleman at a cookery demonstration who wished to see the room behind the Aga as he was convinced that I could not produce so much food from a two-oven Aga in the time. Needless to say he didn't manage to find the secret hatch to another cooker

USING YOUR AGA

All the following recipes give specific cooking instructions, so even if you are new to Aga ownership you should find getting to know your Aga fairly simple. But here are a few hints and tips to help you get the most from your Aga. I learn so much from meeting other Aga owners, those that come to spend the day with me doing a cookery course as well as all the customers I meet in Aga showrooms.

Whether or not your Aga is shiny new or a cherished older model a few basics will help you get the most from it. An Aga is really a storage heater that releases stored heat gently into the ovens. As soon as the lids are lifted then the stored heat will be used quickly, so the basic principle is to use the oven heat as much as possible. This is something that new owners find difficult at first. Try cooking rice or potatoes by the method described above and you will see that using the oven is simple and saves pans of water boiling over and steam filling the kitchen.

As there is no single source of heat in the oven, food can be placed against the sides and back of each oven. The floor of the roasting oven is useful to bake pastry cases on as well as pies, and you can put a frying pan on it for frying onions. As the ovens are fully vented there is no cross-flavouring of food being cooked together in the oven.

The two hotplates are also fairly versatile. The boiling plate is used to boil the kettle (pointing the spout towards the lid directs the steam onto the inside of the lid and helps to keep it clean) and pans of boiling water. Making toast, using the characteristic Aga toast bat, is also done on this plate. Pre-heating the bat before putting the bread in will help prevent the bread from sticking. The wok and ridged pan are heated and used on this plate also. The simmering plate is the place where sauces are made, toasted sandwiches are toasted, drop scones and naan breads are cooked. Do not be tempted to cook any food with a lot of fat in it directly on the metal plates, the fat will burn and any excess will run into the insulation.

Give these plates a regular brush with a wire brush to remove crumbs and boiled over food. These little bits can slow the cooking in a saucepan or the boiling of a kettle.

Wipe over the black enamel top after every use and it will remain in good condition. The occasional clean with a damp cloth and Astonish paste should keep the Aga looking clean. The shiny chrome or stainless steel lids can be cleaned with a stainless steel cleaner or Bar Keepers Friend.

More details on how to clean the Aga when it is off for servicing can be found in my *Traditional Aga Cookery Book*.

BREADS

INTRODUCTION

When I was teaching Home Economics I always really enjoyed the bread-making lessons; the children had fun and gained such pleasure from the results. I always taught them to remember that yeast is a living organism, as they were, and needs the same things for survival and growth; i.e. food, warmth, air and moisture.

INGREDIENTS FOR BREAD MAKING

There are many different types of flour used in bread making available from a number of suppliers. Supermarkets now stock a good range of high quality flours and are a good basic source of supply. What follows is a simple guide to choosing flour:

WHEAT FLOURS

Strong flour is often milled from Canadian wheat. 'Strong' refers to the protein content of the wheat. To get the correct texture of bread, the flour needs to have a high protein content to help develop the stretchiness of the dough during kneading. Always look for 'Strong' on the packet and for an indication that the flour is suitable for bread making. Different millers will use different wording.

Wholemeal flour is used to make brown bread, sometimes referred to by the American term 'wholewheat'. It is flour that contains the whole of the grain, and all the wheatgerm and bran from the grain that is removed when white flour is milled. Wholemeal flour will produce a close textured bread, though you can mix it with white flour to produce a lighter texture.

Bleaching. In this country we have developed the idea that 'white' flour, and therefore white bread, should be *very* 'white'. To achieve this, some flours from the large commercial millers will have been bleached. If you are not too fussy about how white your bread is, then I recommend using unbleached flour for a better flavour.

'**Stoneground**' refers to the method of rolling the wheat to make flour. This method generates less heat during milling, so there is less enzyme damage thus resulting in less damage to the wheat germ. This gives a better texture to the bread.

OTHER GRAIN FLOURS

Rye flour has a distinctive taste and is widely used in the production of crisp-breads and dark breads. It produces dense bread but can be mixed with wheat flour for lighter bread. **Spelt flour** dates back to Roman times; some people believe that it has health giving properties. It is popular for it's flavour. **Buckwheat,** regarded as a cereal, is the fruit of a plant belonging to the dock family, native to Russia and China. It has a pleasant nutty flavour and is often used for pancakes and blinis. **Malthouse** flour is a blend of malts mixed with wheat flour to give a distinctive flavour and texture. **Maize,** from which cornmeal and cornflour are produced, is used to make tortillas, cornbreads and polenta.

ORGANIC FLOURS

Organic flours are becoming more widely available, with many of the smaller millers trying to source organic wheat and other grains. However, these are not always available in the quantities needed, although the supply of organic flour does seem to be increasing steadily. I try to use Shipton Mill's stoneground flour which, although not always available organically, does have a wonderful texture.

A word of warning: don't buy too much flour at a time unless you have cool, dry storage. It is always best to use flour as fresh as possible.

Yeast

Yeast is the most frequently used raising agent for bread. Fresh yeast has the best flavour and is readily available from bakers, supermarket bakeries and from health food stores. The yeast is sold as a brown, compressed lump that crumbles easily. It can be stored wrapped in a plastic bag in the fridge for up to two weeks. If it smells rancid, or becomes dry or mouldy, then discard it. I like to blend the yeast with a few grains of sugar and a drop of tepid water. If you then stand the bowl on the Aga, the yeast will soon become active and frothy. It will then be ready to use.

Dried yeast can be substituted for fresh, if preferred. Use half the amount of dried yeast per weight of fresh yeast specified in the ingredients.

Another useful standby is the fast-action or easy-blend yeast sold in measured sachets or small packets. Follow the instructions on the pack; the yeast should be added dry to the flour and not blended with water first. All packs give recommended quantities depending on the amount of flour being used.

Salt

Salt is essential to bring out the flavour of bread. Too much salt will slow the action of the yeast or even kill it, so keep closely to the recipe. I like the flavour of Maldon Sea Salt, either in flakes or ground, but this is a personal preference.

Liquids for bread making

Water is the most frequently used liquid in bread making. Some purists like to use bottled water, and indeed it may be desirable for sour doughs if your water is heavily chlorinated, though I use boiled tap water for my bread making which I think is fine. The most important point to remember is that the liquid is better on the cooler side rather than too hot. The yeast can easily be killed or made dormant right at the beginning of the bread making process if the liquid is over hot. It should be at blood temperature - dip your finger in to test it. If you don't feel confident use cool water.

FATS AND OTHER INGREDIENTS

Oils and fats can add flavour and slightly lengthen the keeping quality of the bread. Small amounts of butter can be rubbed into the flour before the yeast is added, while melted fats and oils can be added with the liquid. However, if a lot of fat is to be incorporated, remember that it will coat the particles of flour and stop the yeast fungus getting to the starch sugars that are its food. Therefore, for example, in a recipe for a rich brioche one should allow time for the yeast to be set aside with the flour just before the fat is added.

Spices are usually added to the flour at the beginning, but items like dried fruits, nuts and olives are best added after the first kneading. If you are kneading your dough in a mixer then remember that the dough hook, or even the blades in the processor, will chop the flavourings which won't allow you to achieve the ideal texture.

GLAZING AND TOPPINGS

Most glazes are used to give a golden, shiny appearance to the finished loaf or rolls. When brushing them on before baking you will need to be very gentle to avoid the crust getting damaged. It is for this reason that I suggest leaving the bread to rise for a further 5 minutes after glazing and before baking. Take care not to get the glaze on the tin, as this will prevent the dough from rising any further and make getting the bread out of the tin more difficult.

There are four types of glaze that I use:

Beaten egg with a pinch of salt and 1 tablespoon of water
gives a shiny, golden finish and crispy crust

Egg yolk beaten with a good pinch of salt
will give a harder finish

2 teaspoons sea salt dissolved in 125ml/$1/4$ pint hot water
will give a paler crust but is good for breads such as French
baguettes that need glazing during the baking process

3 tablespoons of caster sugar and 4 tablespoons
of milk dissolved in a pan and brought to the boil
gives a wonderful sticky finish to sweet doughs and is applied
as soon as the dough is baked and removed from the oven.

There are, of course, many different glazes that you can search out
in other specialist bread books.

Toppings can add variety and texture. They are often added after
the final shaping but before the final rising. Glaze the top and then
either roll the dough in the topping or sprinkle the topping over.
Toppings of choice might include seeds, nuts, herbs, cracked wheat,
sea salt and oats, to name the most common few. Keep an eye on the
bread during baking as these toppings can brown quickly. If they are
browning too quickly, either slide over a sheet of foil or put the cold
shelf on the second set of runners from the top of the oven (this may
slow the cooking, so adjust your baking time accordingly).

SHAPING LOAVES AND ROLLS

Using a basic bread mix – brown or white – your dough can be shaped into a variety of loaves and rolls. Allow the dough to have its first rising and then form the shapes. The shapes listed below can be used for individual portion rolls or loaves. If making rolls, divide the dough into even portions before shaping. I find this easiest to do by forming the dough into a circular shape and then cutting into, say 8 portions. You should grease and flour a large baking tray ready to put your bread on once shaped.

BLOOMER

Roll the dough to an oblong shape, using a rolling pin. Roll up the dough tightly, starting at the shortest end, like a Swiss roll. Lay the loaf on the prepared baking tray with the join side underneath. Using a very sharp knife, cut diagonal slits in the top of the loaf. Dust well with flour. Rise, glaze and bake in the usual way.

COBURG

If using the standard quantity, as above, then divide the dough into two. Form each portion into two round loaves. To do this, place the portion of dough on a lightly floured worktop. Pull the dough from the side up to the middle of the dough. Turn the dough a quarter turn and repeat. Continue to do this until the underside, which will be the top of the loaf, is smooth. Turn the loaf over and place on the prepared baking tray. Using a sharp knife, slash a deep cross across the centre. Dust well with flour. Put to rise, then glaze and bake in the usual way.

COTTAGE LOAF

Cut off one third of the dough. Shape the larger piece into a smooth round loaf, as described for the Coburg loaf. Place on the prepared baking tray. Shape the smaller piece of dough onto a smooth round loaf and place on top of the larger loaf. Flour your forefinger and plunge it through the centre of the two loaves, from top to bottom. This will join the two portions together. Using a sharp knife, score around the edge of the bottom portion of the loaf. Repeat on the top portion of the loaf. Allow the loaf to rise and then glaze and bake.

PLAIT

Divide the dough into three equal portions and roll each portion into a sausage shape. Place the three sausages on the prepared baking tray in parallel lines. Join the dough together at the top and then plait the three portions together, as if plaiting hair. At the end join the three pieces together. Tuck under the ends to form a neat finish. Allow to rise and glaze in the usual way.

SNAIL TWIST

Roll the dough on the worktop into a long sausage shape. Place one end on the prepared baking tray and coil the dough round into a snail shape, twisting the sausage of dough as you coil. Tuck the end under the loaf. Allow to rise and then glaze the dough before baking.

EQUIPMENT

The best piece of equipment for breadmaking is the Aga! There is always somewhere to allow the dough to rise over a steady, gentle heat. And, of course, the roasting oven is just perfect for baking bread. Bread needs a good hot oven to give a crisp crust, so when baking yeast dough choose a time when the oven is up to temperature, not at the end of a cooking session. The all-round Aga heat bakes the bread evenly. In order to get a good even bake, put the shelf on the bottom set of runners of the roasting oven, no higher or the crust will be cooked before the dough is cooked on the inside.

ELECTRIC MIXER OR FOOD PROCESSOR

Many people like to make their bread by hand and find the kneading therapeutic. I have to admit that I nearly always make mine in my **Kitchen Aid mixer**. This speeds up the process, especially the kneading. You will need to use a heavy-duty, free-stand mixer for making any reasonable quantity of bread dough. If you are new to bread making I suggest you stop and feel the dough at various stages and make sure that it is the right consistency i.e. not too moist or too dry. Even if you are an old hand at bread making, I still feel it's important to be able to feel the dough; for this reason, and although I have made bread dough in my very large **Magimix processor**, and the bread is certainly very quickly made, my preference is for a free-standing mixer.

BAKING TRAYS AND TINS

Throughout the recipes in this book I have used the **Aga baking trays** – large and small – that fit onto the runners of the Aga ovens. These baking trays are invaluable because they are a good size and don't warp. Either grease and flour them or line them with Bake-O-Glide.

Loaf tins in various sizes are also essential. Over the last few years I have replaced my old, thin rusty tins with new heavy-duty tins sold in the Aga shops. These have made a real difference to my bread making as now the baked loaf slides out so easily. Always dry the tins well on the Aga after use.

TRIVETS, CHEF'S PADS AND TEA-TOWELS

The top of the Aga is wonderfully warm and certainly the best place to leave the dough to prove or rise. However, it is necessary to protect not just the lids from getting scratched, but also the dough from getting too hot, so use either a **trivet**, an **Aga Chef's Pad** or a folded tea-towel to stand the bowl and the tins on.

BASIC LOAF

A good 'every-day' loaf and one for those new to bread making. Remember to source the best flour and allow enough time for each stage. Once you've enjoyed your first success you'll realise just how easy it is. And so the family's demands for more will begin!

350g/12oz unbleached white bread flour
350g/12oz stoneground wholemeal flour
1 teaspoon crushed sea salt
15g/1/2oz fresh yeast
500ml/18fl oz tepid water

Lightly grease and flour a large baking tray.

Measure the flour and salt into a large mixing bowl. Crumble the yeast into a basin and blend with a little tepid water. Sprinkle over a few grains of sugar or a pinch of flour. Stand the basin on a warm spot on the Aga until the mixture begins to bubble.

Pour the frothy yeast mixture into the flour and add half the measured water. Using either your hand or the dough hook in a food processor, gradually mix the yeast and flour together adding more water as necessary to make a smooth and springy dough which comes cleanly from the bowl. Turn the dough onto a lightly floured work surface and pull and stretch the dough for 10 minutes to make it smooth and elastic. This kneading can be done in a Kitchen Aid mixer and will take about 5 minutes.

Return the dough to the bowl having first lightly oiled it. Cover with either a damp tea-towel or oiled cling film. Stand the bowl either near the Aga or place a trivet or Chef's Pad on the simmering plate lid and stand the bowl on top. Allow the dough to rise until it has doubled in size, this will take about 30-40 minutes. Turn the dough out onto a lightly floured surface and form into an oval shape.

Place the dough lengthways in front of you on the work surface. Pull the long sides together with your fingers and thumb and rock the dough back and forth to make a smooth surface. The crease along the top will become the bottom of the loaf. Turn the loaf into the prepared tin, crease side down. Cover again with a damp tea-towel and return to the top of the Aga and allow to rise until doubled in size.

Sprinkle with a little flour and bake the loaf. Hang the tin on the bottom set of runners of the roasting oven and bake for 25-30 minutes. When baked the loaf should sound hollow when tapped on the bottom and have a golden crust. Cool on a cooling rack.

PLAIN WHITE LOAF

This is another good basic loaf that can be flavoured or shaped in many different ways.

700g/1½lbs unbleached white bread flour
1 teaspoon crushed sea salt
15g/½oz fresh yeast
500ml/18fl oz tepid water

Lightly grease and flour a 1kg (2lb) loaf tin.

Measure the flour and salt into a large mixing bowl. Crumble the yeast into a small basin and blend with a little tepid water. Sprinkle in a pinch of flour or sugar and stand on the Aga until frothing.

Pour the yeast into the flour and mix with most but not all of the water, either by hand or in a food processor, to form a dough that is not at all floury, but slightly sticky and manageable. Turn out onto a lightly floured work surface and either knead for 10 minutes by hand or in a food processor for 5 minutes until smooth and elastic. Place the dough in a lightly oiled mixing bowl and cover with either a damp tea-towel or lightly oiled cling film. Stand the bowl near the Aga or on a Chef's Pad on top of the simmering plate and allow to rise until doubled in size. This will take at least 40 minutes. The longer the rising takes, the better the flavour and texture of the loaf will be.

Once the dough has risen, tip onto a lightly floured work surface. Gently knock back and form into a shape similar to that of the loaf tin. Roll the dough tightly, like a Swiss roll, starting at the short end. Place in the tin, join side down. Cover with a damp tea-towel and allow to rise until doubled in size. Do not allow over-rising or the loaf will collapse in the oven.

Either dust the loaf with flour or glaze with a little beaten egg. Cut a slit along the top and allow to rise for a further 5 minutes.

Hang the shelf on the bottom set of runners of the roasting oven. Slide in the loaf tin and leave in the middle of the shelf. Bake for 25-30 minutes, until evenly golden on the top and the loaf sounds hollow when tapped on the bottom. Remove from the tin. If the bread seems a little moist, return the loaf to the oven, directly on the shelf without the tin, for 5-10 minutes. Cool on a wire rack.

This loaf will keep for 3 to 4 days or will freeze for up to a month.

Makes 1 large loaf

MILK BREAD

Milk bread was a real treat when we were growing up. It was unusual for us to have commercially baked bread, but when we did we often had the round milk bread loaves. The home-made variety, although not quite the same, is still a tasty, close-textured loaf.

700g/1¹/₂lbs strong plain flour
1 teaspoon crushed sea salt
15g/¹/₂oz fresh yeast
25g/1oz butter
500ml/18fl oz milk
1 egg

Measure the flour and salt into a mixing bowl. In a separate bowl, blend the yeast with a little milk to form a smooth paste. Pour the remaining milk into a saucepan and add the butter, stand it on the simmering plate and warm slightly. Take care not to get the milk any warmer than tepid or it will take ages to cool down!

Pour the yeast and most of the milk and butter mixture into the flour and work well to make a smooth, slightly sticky dough, adding more milk as needed. Knead well for 8-10 minutes, until the dough is smooth and stretchy. Return to the bowl and cover with a damp tea-towel or lightly oiled cling film. Stand on a trivet or Chef's Pad on or near the Aga until doubled in size.

Grease and flour 2 x 500g (1lb) loaf tins.

When the dough has risen, place on a lightly floured work surface and cut in half. Shape each half into a loaf and place, join side down, in a prepared tin. Cover with a damp tea-towel or oiled cling film and put to rise on top of the Aga. As the dough comes to the top of the tin, lightly glaze with an egg wash and leave to rise again until just above the tin.

Hang the oven shelf on the bottom set of runners in the roasting oven, slide in the loaves and bake for 20-25 until golden brown and sounding hollow when tapped. Remove from the tins. If you like a crust on your loaf, return it to the oven without the tins for a further 5 minutes. Cool on a wire rack.

Makes 2 small loaves

A GOOD WHOLEMEAL LOAF

To produce a really good wholemeal loaf, you need good quality flour such as Shipton Mill's 100% Wholemeal Flour which gives a delicious flavour. For an even nuttier flavour and great texture try their Extra Coarse Wholemeal Flour.

700g/1½lbs stoneground wholemeal flour
3 teaspoons sea salt
15g/½oz fresh yeast
425ml/¾ pint tepid water
1 tablespoon melted butter or vegetable oil

Measure the flour and salt into a mixing bowl. Place the yeast into a basin and blend with a little warm water. Add the yeast mixture and the melted butter or oil to the flour. Work together to form a pliable dough, adding more water if necessary. Knead the dough well for about 10 minutes until the dough has become smooth and elastic.

Place the dough in an oiled bowl and cover with oiled cling film or a lid. Place on the Aga, either on a trivet or Chef's Pad, and allow to rise until doubled in size.

Turn the dough onto a lightly floured worktop and gently knock back. You can make 1 or 2 loaves or rolls from this quantity. I personally find that I get a better bake if I make two loaves rather than one large one. Shape the dough into round loaves and place on a large baking tray either greased and floured or lined with Bake-O-Glide. Cover with a damp tea-towel and put to rise until doubled in size.

Hang the tray on the bottom set of runners of the roasting oven. Bake the loaves for 30 minutes. If they begin to brown too much, slide in the cold shelf on the second set of runners from the top and bake for another 5-10 minutes. When cooked the loaf should sound hollow when tapped on the bottom. Cool on a wire rack.

Makes 1 large loaf or 2 smaller loaves

THE GRANT LOAF

This was first published in a book by by Doris Grant in 1944 to encourage us all to make bread at home. The method is quick and easy and is ideal for beginners. It's a moist wholemeal loaf that keeps well.

700g/1½lbs stoneground wholemeal flour
1 teaspoon salt
15g/½oz yeast
1 teaspoon soft brown sugar
600ml/1 pint lukewarm water

Grease and flour either a 1kg (2lb) loaf tin or 2 x 500g (1lb) loaf tins.

Place the flour and salt in a mixing bowl. In a separate bowl, blend the yeast and a little water together to make a paste. Add the sugar. Stand on or near the Aga until the yeast begins to froth. Add the yeast and remaining water to the flour and stir. Carry on mixing until the dough comes away from the sides of the bowl. Put the dough into the prepared tin and cover with either a damp tea-towel or oiled cling film, and leave until the loaf has risen to within 1cm (½ inch) of the rim of the tin.

Hang the shelf on the bottom set of runners of the roasting oven. Put in the loaf and bake for 40-45 minutes. If you are making two smaller loaves they may bake in 30-35 minutes. When the bread is cooked the loaf should sound hollow when tapped on the bottom. Remove from the tin and cool on a wire rack.

Makes 1 large or 2 small loaves

MALTED GRAIN LOAF

The malted grains in this flour give a wonderful flavour and a nutty texture to the bread. You will find this has more body to it than a commercially made granary loaf.

700g/1¹/₂lbs Malthouse flour with malted grains
2 teaspoons salt
15g/¹/₂oz yeast
425ml/³/₄ pint tepid water
1 tablespoon vegetable oil

Measure the flour into a mixing bowl and add the salt. In a separate bowl, blend the yeast with a little water and add this to the flour. Add the oil and pour in most of the water. Mix the dough, adding the remaining water as needed, until it comes cleanly away from the sides of the bowl and all the flour has been included. The dough should be slightly sticky but manageable at this stage. Knead well for 5-10 minutes. Place the dough in a clean bowl and cover with either a damp tea-towel or oiled cling film. Stand on either a trivet or a Chef's Pad on the simmering plate lid and leave to rise until doubled in size.

Grease and flour 2 x ¹/₂kg (1lb) loaf tins.

Gently knock back the risen dough and cut into two pieces. Shape each half into a loaf and place into a prepared loaf tin. (This bread dough also makes a very nice Cottage loaf.) Re-cover and return to the top of the Aga and allow to rise until the dough is just above the sides of the tin.

Put the oven shelf on the bottom set of runners of the roasting oven. Put in the risen loaves and bake for 25-30 minutes, until golden brown and sounding hollow when tapped. Cool on a wire rack.

Makes 2 small loaves

FLOURY ROLLS

My son Hugo loves soft fluffy rolls made by commercial bakeries. I think they are more like cotton wool in taste and texture. Here is my home-made version, not quite so fluffy but with much more flavour!

450g/1lb strong white flour
1 teaspoon salt
15g/¹/₂oz yeast
150ml/5fl oz water
150ml/5fl oz warm milk
a little extra flour to dust

Measure the flour and salt into a mixing bowl. In a separate bowl, blend the yeast with a little water and add to the flour. Pour in the liquid and knead to make a pliable dough, adding more water if necessary. Knead the dough well for 10 minutes, until smooth and stretchy. Place the dough in a lightly oiled bowl and cover with oiled cling film or a damp tea-towel and place on a trivet or Chef's Pad on the Aga to rise until doubled in size.

Tip the risen dough on to a lightly floured work top and gently knock back. Divide the dough into 10 even portions and shape each one into a ball. Gently roll each ball with a rolling pin to make an oval shape, about 10cm (4 inches) long. Place on a greased and floured baking tray, close enough for them to touch when risen.

Place the baking tray on a trivet or Chef's Pad on top of the Aga. Cover with oiled cling film and leave to rise until doubled in size. Dust the tops of the rolls with a little flour. Put the baking tray on the second set of runners from the bottom of the roasting oven. If you have water spray handy, then spray the top of the rolls with water when they first go in the oven, repeating after 5 minutes. Bake for 15-20 minutes until lightly coloured and slightly hollow sounding when tapped on the bottom. Slide them off the baking tray onto a cooling rack and cover with a clean tea-towel whilst they cool.

Makes 10 rolls

PAIN DE MIE OR SANDWICH LOAF

This loaf has a slightly rich, soft interior that makes it good both for sandwiches and to use for a bread and butter pudding!

700g/1¹/₂lbs strong white flour
2 teaspoons salt
50g/2oz butter
25g/1oz yeast
250ml/8fl oz milk
2 tablespoons semolina

Measure the flour, salt and butter into a mixing bowl and rub the butter into the flour until it resembles breadcrumbs. In a separate bowl, blend the yeast with some of the milk to make a smooth paste. Add this to the flour mixture and enough milk to make a firm dough. Knead the dough to make it smooth, silky and stretchy. Place the dough in a mixing bowl and cover with a damp tea-towel or oiled cling film. Stand the bowl on a trivet on top of the Aga and leave until the dough has doubled in size.

Grease and flour or line a large baking tray with Bake-O-Glide.

Turn the dough out onto a lightly floured worktop and lightly knock back. Shape the dough into either 1 large or two smaller oval shaped loaves. Place the loaves on the prepared baking tray and brush with water. Scatter the semolina over. Stand the baking tray on a trivet on top of the Aga. Cover the bread loosely with a tea-towel and leave to rise until nearly doubled in size.

Hang the baking tray on the bottom set of runners of the roasting oven and bake for 30-35 minutes for a large loaf and 25-30 minutes for a small one, until the bread is golden brown and the loaf sounds hollow when tapped on the bottom. Cool on a wire rack.

Makes 1 large loaf or 2 small loaves

OVERNIGHT BREAD

Leaving the dough overnight allows more time for the yeast to ferment thus adding flavour to the bread, which is one of the reasons bakeries sell 'overnight bread' at a premium price. This method also works well for rolls and shallow bread. The dough needs to be left in the fridge, so do remember to leave enough room.

450g/1lb strong white flour
2 teaspoons salt
25g/1oz butter
15g/¹/₂oz fresh yeast
300ml/¹/₂ pint water

Place the flour, salt and butter in a mixing bowl and rub in the butter until the mixture resembles breadcrumbs. Blend the yeast with a little water and add to the flour along with most of the water. Mix together to make a slightly soft dough, adding more water as needed. Knead the dough well until smooth and pliable. Place in a mixing bowl and cover with oiled cling film or a damp tea-towel. Stand on a trivet on the Aga and leave to rise until doubled in volume.

Grease and flour a 23cm (9 inch) cake tin. Knock back the dough and divide into 8 portions. Shape each into a roll and place 7 round the edge of the tin and one in the middle. Brush with egg wash or milk for a glazed bread. Cover loosely with oiled cling film and place in the fridge overnight.

In the morning, hang the oven shelf on the bottom set of runners of the roasting oven and slide in the bread straight from the fridge. Bake for 20-25 minutes. Remove from the oven when golden brown and sounding hollow when tapped. Cool on a wire rack before serving.

Makes 1 loaf or 8 rolls

FRENCH STICKS OR BAGUETTES

Baguettes are remarkably easy to make at home and are far superior to any that you can buy in the average high street. I use Shipton Mill's French white flour which helps achieve the right texture. If you can't find Shipton's then use 3/4 strong white flour and 1/4 white flour.

450g/1lb French white flour
2 teaspoons sea salt
15g/1/2oz fresh yeast
325ml/11fl oz water

For the glaze
3 teaspoons sea salt dissolved in 125ml/1/4 pint hot water

Place the flour and salt in a mixing bowl. Blend the yeast in a small basin with a little water. Add the yeast and the water to the flour and work together to make a dough, adding more water if needed to ensure the dough isn't too dry. Knead well for about 10 minutes until the dough is smooth and stretchy. Place the dough in an oiled bowl, cover with oiled cling film and stand on a trivet or Chef's Pad until risen to double in size.

Tip the risen dough onto a lightly floured worktop and cut in half. Roll one half into an oblong about 30 x 15 cm (12 x 6 inches). Have the longest end nearer you, fold one third of the dough up to the middle and then overlap the top third. Cover and leave to rest for 10 minutes. Turn the dough and repeat the process twice more. Do the same with the other half of dough.

Shape the dough by rolling it on the work top into a sausage shape about 30cm (12 inches) long. Lay the dough on a well floured linen tea-towel, pleating the towel between each loaf. Cover with a damp tea-towel and leave to rise until doubled in size. Gently roll onto a greased and floured baking tray or one lined with Bake-O-Glide. Make several diagonal slashes in the top of each loaf using a sharp knife. Brush with the salt water glaze.

Hang the tray on the second set of runners from the bottom of the roasting oven and bake the baguettes for 10 minutes. Re-glaze the bread and return the tray to the bottom set of runners of the roasting oven and bake for a further 20-25 minutes, until the loaves are crisp and brown and sound hollow when tapped on the bottom. Cool on a wire rack. Best served warm and freshly baked.

Makes 2 French sticks

BAGELS

These Jewish rolls have become very popular over the last few years. They have a slightly chewy texture and are excellent when buttered or filled with cream cheese. Any not eaten fresh can be halved and then toasted.

450g/1lb strong plain flour
2 teaspoons salt
15g/¹/₂oz yeast
300ml/10fl oz water and milk mixed, at room temperature
1 teaspoon sugar
2 tablespoons vegetable oil
1 egg, separated
sesame and poppy seeds

Measure the flour and salt into a mixing bowl. In a separate bowl blend the yeast with a little of the water and milk mixture and add this to the flour along with the sugar and vegetable oil.

In a separate bowl, beat the egg white until white and frothy but not stiff. Add to the flour mixture. Mix, adding enough liquid to form a firm, pliable dough. Knead well for 5-10 minutes until the dough is smooth and stretchy. Place in an oiled bowl and cover with oiled cling film and put on a trivet on top of the Aga. Leave to rise until doubled in size.

Tip the dough onto a floured worktop and form into a ball. Divide into 16 even portions. Shape each portion into a roll and press your thumb through the centre of the roll. Enlarge the hole slightly by turning your thumb round several times in the hole. Place on a greased baking tray or one lined with Bake-O-Glide. Stand the tray on a trivet on top of the Aga and cover with a damp tea-towel. Leave the bagels to rise until doubled in volume.

To cook the bagels, boil a large pan of water then transfer the pan to the simmering plate. Using a straining spoon slide the bagel into the water, 2 or 3 at a time. Poach for about 30 seconds until the bagel floats to the top. Return the bagel to the baking tray. Continue until all the bagels have been poached.

For the glaze, mix the egg yolk with 2 teaspoons of cold water and brush it over the bagels. Sprinkle over some poppy or sesame seeds. They are now ready for baking.

Hang the shelf on the bottom set of runners of the roasting oven and bake for 20-25 minutes, until golden brown and puffed up. Cool on a wire rack.

Makes 16

PITTA BREADS

These little breads are so easy to make and so much tastier than the ones that supermarkets sell. They are very versatile and freeze well, so it's worth making plenty at a time. They can also be made with wholemeal flour, though you may need to add a little extra water.

450g/1lb strong white flour
1 teaspoon salt
15g/1/2oz yeast
300ml/1/2 pint tepid water
1 tablespoon olive oil

Measure the flour and the salt into a mixing bowl. In a separate bowl blend together the yeast and a little water to make a smooth paste. Add the yeast mixture to the flour along with the olive oil and most of the liquid. Knead to a soft, smooth dough, adding the remaining water as needed. Knead well until the dough is smooth and silky. Cover with a damp tea-towel or oiled cling film and stand on a trivet on the Aga to rise to double in size.

Turn onto a lightly floured worktop and divide the dough into 12 portions. Form each portion into balls as you would with bread rolls. Leave the balls on the floured worktop and cover with a damp tea-towel or oiled cling film for 5-10 minutes.

Roll the balls out with a rolling pin to circles about 15cm (6 inches) in diameter. They need to be about 0.5cm (1/4 inch) thick, if they are too thin they will be like biscuits when cooked. Place the breads on prepared baking trays and leave to rise until doubled in volume. Slide one tray of pitta breads onto the third set of runners from the top of the roasting oven. Bake for 2-3 minutes. They should be risen and puffy but not browning. If they begin to brown, move the shelf to the bottom set of runners for 1-2 minutes. When firm and dry, transfer to a wire rack and cover with a dry tea-towel. Cook the remaining breads. Serve slit and filled or torn into pieces to serve with a mezze such as aubergine paté or hummus.

Makes 12 breads

SODA BREAD

Although soda bread does not actually contain yeast it is still thought of as bread. It's delicious to have for breakfast and is especially good with crispy bacon and fried eggs, though I particularly like it with marmalade and butter. It doesn't keep well but can be frozen.

350g/12oz wholemeal flour
110g/4 oz plain white flour
1 teaspoon salt
1 level teaspoon bicarbonate of soda
50g/2oz butter
225ml/8fl oz milk
150g/5oz plain yoghurt

Measure the flours, salt and bicarbonate of soda into a mixing bowl. Add the butter and rub into the flour until the mixture resembles breadcrumbs. Add the milk and yoghurt and mix to a soft dough. Knead the dough very lightly on a floured worktop and then shape the dough into a round about 2.5cm (1 inch) thick and place on a prepared baking tray. Using a sharp knife, cut a cross in the top.

Hang the baking tray on the bottom set of runners of the roasting oven and bake the loaf for 35-45 minutes, until the loaf is crusty and brown and sounds hollow when tapped underneath. Cool on a wire rack.

BREAD STICKS OR GRISSINI

Bread sticks are very easy to make and are so much better than their commercial namesakes. For this recipe I have used wholemeal flour but you can use white flour or a mixture of both. They keep well for a week or two in a tin.

450g/1lb wholemeal bread flour
2 teaspoons salt
15g/¹⁄₂oz fresh yeast
250ml/8fl oz warm water
3 tablespoons olive oil

Some variations
50g/2oz grated Parmesan cheese,
added to the flour
1 tablespoon sun-dried tomato paste,
added with the olive oil
2 tablespoons sesame or black poppy seeds,
scattered over the shaped grissini

Measure the flour and salt into a mixing bowl. Place the yeast in a basin and blend with a little water to make a smooth paste. Add the yeast to the flour along with the olive oil and 6 fl oz of the water. Work the dough until it is smooth but firm, adding more water as needed. Place the dough in the mixing bowl and cover with a damp tea-towel or oiled cling film. Stand on a trivet on top of the Aga to rise until doubled in size.

Turn the risen dough out onto a lightly floured work surface and knock back. Cut the dough in half and roll each half into a rectangle about 5mm (¹⁄₄ inch) thick. Cut each rectangle in half to make two rectangles. Cut these rectangles into strips about 1cm (¹⁄₂ inch) wide. Roll the dough, using your hands, into a thin round strip about 20cm (8 inches) long.

Place on a large baking tray, lightly greased or lined with Bake-O-Glide. Immediately after shaping, place the tin on the second set of runners from the top of the roasting oven. Bake for 12-15 minutes until golden brown, and crispy. Cool on a wire rack. Repeat until all the grissini are baked.

Makes about 50 sticks

FOCACCIA

Focaccia is an Italian flat bread now very popular in this country, flavoured with olive oil, salt and occasionally herbs. I sometimes lay a few sprigs of rosemary on the loaf before baking to add flavour - be sure to remove the sprigs before serving as cooked rosemary can be extremely painful to eat!

450g/1lb strong white flour
2 teaspoons salt
4 tablespoons olive oil
15g/1/2oz fresh yeast
300ml/1/2 pint tepid water
1-2 tablespoons olive oil to pour on before baking
scant tablespoon Maldon sea salt for sprinkling

Place the flour, salt and olive oil into a large mixing bowl.

Blend the yeast with a little tepid water in a small basin. Add this to the flour with most of the remaining water. Mix to form a dough that will bind together but is slightly sticky, adding more of the measured water if needed. Knead the dough, either by hand or in a food processor, until stretchy and smooth. Return to a clean bowl and cover with either a damp tea-towel or oiled cling film.

Stand on a trivet or Chef's Pad on or near the Aga and leave to rise until doubled in size.

Oil a baking tray approximately 40 x 28cm (15 x 11 inches). When the dough has risen, tip onto a lightly floured work surface and gently knock back the dough. Roll out to fit the oiled baking tray. Cover again and leave to rise. When the dough has doubled in size press your spaced fingers all over the surface of the dough to form indentations taking care not to make a hole in the dough. Drizzle over the olive oil and scatter over the coarse sea salt.

Hang the shelf on the bottom set of runners of the roasting oven, put in the focaccia and bake for 25-30 minutes, until golden brown all over and sounding hollow when tapped. Turn out onto a cooling rack.

This loaf is best eaten warm.

Makes 1 large loaf

CIABATTA

This fashionable, light bread is supposed to resemble a slipper shape when baked. It takes a long time to make, hence its high price at the bakers. It doesn't need a lot of attention, so just make it on a day when you are going to be around the kitchen. Use ciabatta flour, if available, which is slightly coarser than ordinary strong flour and will help you to achieve the characteristic air bubbles in the bread. Like so many breads in this book, any extra loaves will freeze well.

700g/1¹/₂lbs Shipton Mill ciabatta flour
2 teaspoons salt
15g/¹/₂oz fresh yeast
150ml/¹/₄ pint olive oil
425ml/³/₄ pint cold water

Measure the flour and salt into a mixing bowl. In a separate bowl, blend the yeast with a little water and add to the flour. Pour in the olive oil and most of the water. Mix, adding the remaining water if possible, whilst still keeping the dough manageable. The flour will absorb the water during the long rising process. Knead the dough well until smooth and elastic. Place the dough in a large, oiled mixing bowl. Cover with oiled cling film or a lid and leave in the warm kitchen, but not on the Aga, to rise for 2-3 hours until the dough has doubled in size. Knock back again and set to rise again in the same way until again doubled in size.

Grease and flour or line with Bake-O-Glide, two large baking trays. When the dough has doubled in volume, carefully cut the dough in half while it is still in the bowl. Gently tip each portion onto the prepared baking tray. The dough should form into a long, rough oblong or slipper shape, about 2.5cm (1 inch) thick. Dust the top with flour and put the baking trays on trivets on top of the Aga and leave to rise again until doubled in volume. Bake on the second set of runners from the bottom of the roasting oven for 25-30 minutes, until lightly browned and sounding hollow when tapped.

Makes 2 loaves

CHALLAH

This is a traditional, enriched loaf eaten on the Jewish Sabbath. It is usually plaited with between four and twelve strands of dough, highly glazed and dusted with poppy seeds. I especially like this loaf as it is not quite so rich as a brioche and has a slightly closer texture.

600g/1¼lbs strong plain flour
2 tablespoons caster sugar
1 teaspoon salt
15g/½oz yeast
225ml/8fl oz water
75g/3oz butter, melted
3 eggs
1 egg white
1 egg yolk beaten together with 1 tablespoon
cold water, to glaze
1 tablespoon poppy seeds

Measure the flour, sugar and salt together into a mixing bowl. In a separate bowl, blend the yeast with a little water. Add the yeast mixture and melted butter to the flour and sugar.

In another bowl, beat together the eggs and the egg white and add these to the flour mixture. Mix together, adding more water as necessary to make a smooth, pliable dough. Knead until stretchy. Place the dough in an oiled mixing bowl and cover with a damp tea-towel or oiled cling film. Stand on a trivet on top of the Aga to rise until doubled in size.

Turn the risen dough out onto a lightly floured worktop and divide the mixture into four. Roll the quarters into long ropes, about 30cm (12 inches) long. Place the ropes side by side on a large sheet of Bake-O-Glide, or a floured worktop, and pinch together the four ends furthest away from you. Starting from the right-hand side take the right (or first) rope and lift over the second rope. Take the third rope and lift over the fourth rope. Now take the fourth rope and lift over between the first and second rope. Repeat from the right until the plait is completed. Tuck the ends under and lift onto the large baking tray. This is easier if the plait is on the Bake-O-Glide. Cover with lightly oiled cling film and stand on a trivet and leave to rise on the top of the Aga until doubled in size. Remove the cling film and glaze with the egg yolk mixture. Leave for a further 5 minutes and gently re-glaze and sprinkle over the poppy seeds.

Hang the tray on the bottom set of runners of the roasting oven and bake for 35-40 minutes, until a deep golden brown and sounding hollow when tapped. Cool on a wire rack.

Makes 1 large loaf

HERBED GRANARY STICK

This is a wonderful loaf to serve warm with a cheese and paté lunch.
Fresh herbs are essential.

450g/1lb Granary or Malthouse flour
1 teaspoon salt
2 tablespoons chopped fresh parsley
2 tablespoons chopped fresh herbs e.g. mint, thyme, marjoram,
chives
15g/¹⁄₂oz yeast
300ml/¹⁄₂ pint warm water

Measure the flour, the salt, the chopped parsley and the chopped
mixed herbs into a bowl and stir to mix. In a separate bowl, blend
the yeast with a little water and add this to the flour. Add enough
water to make a slightly sticky dough. Knead the dough until
smooth and stretchy. Place the dough in a bowl and cover with a
damp tea-towel or oiled cling film. Stand the bowl on a trivet on top
of the Aga and leave to rise until doubled in size.

Grease and flour a baking tray or line it with Bake-O-Glide.

Turn the risen dough out onto a lightly floured worktop and cut in
half. Shape each portion into a sausage shape about 25.5cm (10
inches) long and place the loaves on the baking tray. Cover with a
damp tea-towel or oiled cling film and return to the trivet on top of
the Aga and allow the dough to rise until nearly doubled in size.
Diagonally cut the top of each loaf three times with a sharp knife
and brush with a little milk. Hang the tray on the bottom set of
runners of the roasting oven and bake for 20-25 minutes, until
golden brown and sounding hollow when tapped on the bottom.

Makes 2 sticks

SAFFRON BREAD

I have very fond memories of saffron bread. When I was at college, training to be a Home Economics teacher, the mother of one of my friends would make saffron bread at home, then freeze it, wrap it and post it to Bea at college. It arrived beautifully thawed and ready for us to eat!

1 teaspoon saffron strands
2 tablespoons warm water
450g/1lb strong white flour
1 teaspoon salt
75g/3oz sugar
175g/6oz butter, diced
225g/8oz dried fruit e.g. currants, raisins, peel
25g/1oz fresh yeast
200ml/7fl oz warm milk

Place the saffron in a basin and add the warm water. Leave to stand at the back of the Aga for at least 1 hour.

Measure the flour, salt, sugar and butter into a mixing bowl. Rub the butter into the flour until it resembles breadcrumbs and then stir in the dried fruit. In a separate bowl, blend the yeast with some of the milk and add to the flour and fruit mixture. Mix, adding enough milk to form a slightly sticky dough. Knead the dough until stretchy and smooth. Place in a mixing bowl and cover with either a damp tea-towel or oiled cling film. Stand on a trivet on top of the Aga and leave to rise until nearly doubled in volume.

Grease and flour 2 x ½kg (1 lb) loaf tins.

Turn the risen dough onto a lightly floured worktop and gently knock back. Cut the dough in half and shape into two loaves and place in the prepared tins. Cover with oiled cling film or a damp tea-towel and stand on a trivet on top of the Aga. Leave to rise until the loaves have risen to the top of their tins. Place the shelf on the floor of the roasting oven and bake the saffron bread for 30-35 minutes until brown on the top and sounding hollow when tapped.

Leave in the tin for 4 or 5 minutes and then turn out onto a cooling rack.

This mixture can also be used to make saffron buns.

Makes 2 small loaves

SPELT BREAD

Spelt bread is made from the flour of the Spelt grain, a cereal that was popular in Roman Times. It's full of flavour and naturally rich in minerals and is sometimes used by those suffering wheat allergies (check with a dietician first).

450g/1lb spelt flour
2 teaspoons salt
1 tablespoon olive oil
15g/^{1}/$_2$oz yeast
300ml/^{1}/$_2$ pint tepid water

Grease and flour a ^{1}/$_2$kg (1lb) loaf tin.

Measure the flour and salt into a mixing bowl and add the oil. In a separate bowl, blend the yeast with a little water and add to the flour mixture. Add the remaining water and stir to a dough like consistency. The dough will be very wet and slippery compared with other bread dough. Beat the dough either with your hand or in a food processor. Knead the dough until it comes cleanly from the sides of the bowl. When it has become a little more manageable, turn the dough directly into the prepared tin. Push the dough into the corners of the tin using either wet hands or a wet pastry brush.

Stand the loaf tin on a trivet or Chef's Pad on top of the simmering plate lid. Cover with a damp tea-towel and leave to rise until the bread has risen to just below the top of the tin.

Put the shelf on the bottom set of runners of the roasting oven and bake the loaf for 35-40 minutes, until golden brown and sounding hollow when tapped. Remove from the tin and cool on a wire rack.

Makes 1 small loaf

RYE BREAD

Rye bread is full of flavour and has a wonderfully dense texture. Here I have used a combination of Shipton Mill's Light Rye Flour and their strong white flour.

350g/12oz Shipton Mill's Light Rye flour
110g/4oz strong white flour
1 teaspoon salt
1 tablespoon treacle
15g/¹/₂oz yeast
300ml/¹/₂ pint water
poppy seeds, optional

Measure the flours into a mixing bowl and add the salt. In a separate bowl, blend the yeast and treacle with some of the water. Add this mixture to the flours along with the remaining water. Mix the ingredients to make a firm dough. Knead well until the dough is smooth and then cover with either a damp tea-towel or oiled cling film. Stand on a trivet or a Chef's Pad on the Aga and leave to rise until doubled in size.

When the dough is risen, tip onto a lightly floured work top and gently knock back. Shape the dough into an oval shaped loaf and place on a lightly greased and floured baking tray or one lined with Bake-O-Glide. Cover with a damp tea-towel or oiled cling film and put to rise on the Aga until doubled in size.

If finishing with poppy seeds, brush the top of the risen loaf with water and scatter over the seeds.

Hang the tin on the bottom set of runners of the roasting oven and bake the loaf for 30-35 minutes, until a good crust has formed and the loaf sounds hollow when tapped on the bottom. Cool on a wire rack.

Makes 1 loaf

SWISS LOAF

This bread goes very well with cheese. It has the appearance of a rustic loaf, but the texture is even and has an excellent flavour.

450g/1lb Shipton Mill's Dark Swiss flour
1 teaspoon salt
15g/¹/₂oz yeast
250ml/8fl oz milk
250ml/8fl oz plain yoghurt

Measure the flour and salt into a mixing bowl. In a separate bowl, blend the yeast with a little milk to make a runny paste. Add the yeast to the flour along with the yoghurt and most of the milk. Mix all the ingredients together to make a smooth and slightly sticky dough, adding the remaining milk if needed. Knead the dough until smooth and stretchy. Place in a mixing bowl and cover with either a damp tea-towel or oiled cling film. Stand the bowl on a trivet on top of the Aga and leave to rise until the dough has doubled in size.

Grease and flour a large baking tray or line with Bake-O-Glide. Put to one side. Line a mixing bowl with a clean tea-towel and dust well with flour.

Turn the risen dough out onto a lightly floured worktop and gently knock back. Shape into a round loaf and place in the tea-towel lined bowl, with the top of the loaf facing down. Cover the loaf with the overhanging tea-towel and stand on the trivet on top of the Aga to rise until almost doubled in size. Unwrap the loaf and carefully turn out onto the prepared tray. Dust the top with flour. Using a sharp knife, cut 5 slashes horizontally and 5 slashes vertically on top of the loaf. Leave to rise again for 5-10 minutes.

Hang the baking tray on the bottom set of runners of the roasting oven and bake for 25-30 minutes, until the loaf is brown on the top and sounds hollow when tapped on the bottom. Cool.

Makes 1 large loaf

OLIVE BREAD

This is always a popular bread at my demonstrations. It's easy and goes so well with tomatoes and cheese for a simple but delicious lunch.

450g/1lb strong white four
2 teaspoons salt
15g/¹/₂oz fresh yeast
300ml/¹/₂ pint warm water
3 tablespoons olive oil
150g/5oz pitted olives

Measure the flour and salt into a mixing bowl. In a separate bowl, blend the yeast with a little water to make a paste. Add the yeast to the flour with 2 tablespoons of olive oil and most of the water. Work the ingredients to make a soft dough, adding more liquid if necessary. Knead to form a smooth pliable dough. Place in the mixing bowl, cover with a damp tea-towel or oiled cling film and stand on a trivet on top of the Aga until doubled in size.

Turn the dough onto a lightly floured work surface, knock back lightly and then roll out to a rectangular shape, roughly 23 x 30cm (9 x 12 inches). Roughly chop the pitted olives and scatter over the dough. Roll the dough tightly like a Swiss roll.

Use a little of the remaining olive oil to grease the inside of a 1kg (2lb) loaf tin. Tuck the ends of the rolled loaf under the loaf and drop into the oiled tin. Pour the remaining oil over the top of the loaf. Cover the loaf with oiled cling film and stand on a trivet on top of the Aga until the dough has just risen to the top of the tin.

Place the shelf on the floor of the roasting oven and put in the loaf. Bake for 25-30 minutes until golden brown and sounding hollow when tapped. Cool on a wire rack.

Makes 1 large loaf

ROAST GARLIC BREAD

Slightly different to the conventional garlic bread. This is more for lovers of roast garlic and goes really well with simple cheese and hams. If you want to roast the garlic in advance of making the bread, it will keep for a day or two in the fridge.

1 large head of garlic
1 tablespoon olive oil for roasting
350g/12oz strong white flour
1 teaspoon salt
1 tablespoon olive oil
15g/¹⁄₂oz fresh yeast
250ml/8fl oz water
beaten egg, to glaze
2 tablespoons semolina

Place the whole bulb of garlic on a small baking tray and drizzle over the oil. Hang the shelf on the bottom set of runners of the roasting oven and put in the garlic. Roast for 15-20 minutes, until the garlic bulbs are soft but not brown. Remove from the oven and allow to cool.

Place the flour, salt and olive oil in a large mixing bowl. Blend the yeast with a little water to make a runny paste and add to the flour. Add most of the remaining water and mix the dough until soft and pliable, adding more water as necessary. Knead the dough until smooth and elastic. Place the kneaded dough in a mixing bowl and cover either with a damp tea-towel or oiled cling film. Stand the bowl on a trivet on top of the Aga and leave the dough to rise until doubled in volume.

While the dough is rising, break off the bulbs of garlic, snip the top off each clove with a pair of scissors and squeeze out the flesh into a bowl. Lightly mash the cloves together.

Turn the risen dough out onto a lightly floured surface and roll out to a rectangle, roughly 30.5 x 20.5cm (12 x 8 inches). Spread the dough with the mashed garlic – it may be patchy but it doesn't matter. Roll up the dough like a Swiss roll and flatten with your hands.

Grease and flour or line with Bake-O-Glide, a large baking tray. Place the garlic loaf on the tin and pinch together the open ends. Brush with either beaten egg or with water and dust with the semolina.

Stand the tray on a trivet on top of the Aga, cover the bread with a damp tea-towel or oiled cling film. Allow the dough to rise until doubled in size.

Hang the tray or shelf on the bottom set of runners of the roasting oven and bake the loaf for 20-25 minutes, until golden brown and sounding hollow when tapped. Cool on a wire rack.

Makes one large garlic loaf

TOMATO AND OLIVE BUNS

These are like a kind of savoury Chelsea Bun - just add a slice of cheese for a tasty picnic roll.

450g/1lb strong white flour
1 teaspoon salt
2 tablespoons olive oil or oil from a jar of sun-dried tomatoes
15g/½oz yeast
250ml/8fl oz warm water
2 tablespoons sun-dried tomato paste
8 pieces sun-dried tomatoes in oil, finely sliced
10-12 black olives, pitted and roughly chopped

Measure the flour, salt and oil into a mixing bowl. In a separate bowl, blend the yeast with some of the water and add it to the flour. Continue mixing and kneading the dough until all the ingredients have been combined, adding enough water to form a smooth and stretchy dough. Place the dough into a clean bowl and cover either with a damp tea-towel or oiled cling film. Stand the bowl on a trivet on top of the Aga and leave until the dough has doubled in size.

Grease, flour and line the base of a 23cm (9 inch) square cake tin.

Turn the dough out onto a lightly floured worktop and lightly knock back. Roll the dough out to an oblong, roughly 40 x 22.5cm (16 x 9 inches). Spread the sun-dried tomato paste over the dough and scatter over the sun-dried tomato pieces and the chopped olives. Tightly roll the dough up from the longest side in the same way a Swiss roll is made. Divide the roll into 9 even pieces. Place the pieces, cut side uppermost, in the prepared tin. Cover with cling film and stand on a trivet on top of the Aga. Leave to rise until the pieces have begun to merge together.

Hang the shelf on the bottom set of runners of the roasting oven. Remove the cling film from the top of the rolls. Put the tin in the oven on the shelf and bake for 25-30 minutes, until golden brown and hollow when tapped. Cool on a wire rack.

Makes 9 buns

FETA AND OLIVE LOAF

Classic Mediterranean ingredients make this loaf a meal in itself.

350g/12oz strong white flour
1 teaspoon salt
15g/1/2oz yeast
200ml/7fl oz warm water
75g/3oz pitted black olives, halved
75g/3oz feta cheese, cubed
2 tablespoons olive oil

Measure the flour and salt into a mixing bowl. In a separate bowl, blend the yeast with a little water and add to the flour. Stir in the olives and the feta cheese (if you are mixing the dough in a food processor, add the olives and feta cheese after the dough has been made). Mix and knead the flour, adding enough water to form a smooth stretchy dough. After kneading the dough for 5-10 minutes place it in a bowl, cover with either a damp tea-towel or oiled cling film and place on a trivet or Chef's Pad on top of the Aga to rise until doubled in size.

Smear the sides and base of a 25cm (10 inch) round cake tin.

Turn the risen dough onto a lightly floured worktop and gently knock back. Shape into a round and roll out with a rolling pin to a circle to fit the tin. Place the dough in the oiled tin and cover with either a damp tea-towel or oiled cling film and return to the top of the Aga to rise. When risen to double in volume, press the top with the tips of your fingers, gently, to form indentations over the surface of the loaf. Pour over the olive oil.

Hang the shelf on the bottom set of runners of the roasting oven and put in the bread tin. Bake for 25-30 minutes, until golden brown and sounding hollow when tapped on the bottom.

Cool on a wire rack. Best served warm.

SUN-DRIED TOMATO BREAD

I've used a mixture of tomato paste and chopped tomatoes in this recipe but you can use either on its own. If you use tomatoes from a jar you can use the flavoured oil as a substitute for the olive oil.

450g/1lb strong white flour
2 teaspoons salt
15g/¹⁄₂oz yeast
300ml/¹⁄₂ pint warm water
1 tablespoon olive oil
2 tablespoons sun-dried tomato paste
4 pieces sun-dried tomatoes, finely snipped

Measure the flour and salt into a mixing bowl. In a separate basin, blend the yeast with a little water and pour into the flour. Add the olive oil, sun-dried tomato paste and sun-dried tomatoes (if using a food-processor, add the tomatoes at the end of this stage so that they don't get over-chopped). Add about half the water and mix to a dough, adding more water if necessary to make the dough smooth and pliable. Knead well. Place the dough in a mixing bowl and cover with a damp tea-towel or oiled cling film. Stand on a trivet on the Aga and leave to rise until doubled in size.

Turn the risen dough out onto a floured worktop and knock back lightly. Shape the dough into one large loaf and place in an oiled and floured 1kg (2lb) loaf tin or shape into 12 rolls. Place these on a large baking tray, oiled or lined with Bake-O-Glide.

Cover the shaped dough with either oiled cling film or a damp tea-towel and stand on a trivet on top of the Aga to rise to almost doubled in size. Place the shelf on the floor of the roasting oven and slide in the loaf. Bake for 25-30 minutes, until the loaf is golden brown and sounds hollow when tapped. (For the rolls put onto the bottom set of runners in the roasting oven and bake for 20-25 minutes.) Turn onto a wire rack to cool.

Makes 1 large loaf or 12 rolls

CHEESE AND WALNUT LOAF

As walnuts traditionally came from the West Country, I developed this recipe for a special 'Taste of the West' cookery demonstration in Somerset. I used Cheddar cheese, of course, but any flavoursome hard cheese will do. A lovely bread to have with soup.

450g/1lb wholemeal flour
1 teaspoon salt
1 teaspoon paprika powder
1½ teaspoons mustard powder
15g/½oz fresh yeast
300ml/½ pint warm water
110g/4oz Cheddar cheese, grated
110g/4oz walnuts, finely chopped
3 tablespoons finely chopped parsley

For the topping
50g/2oz Cheddar cheese, grated

Grease and flour a 1kg (2lb) loaf tin.

Measure the flour, salt, paprika and mustard powder into a mixing bowl. In a separate bowl, blend the yeast with a little of the warm water and set aside. Stir the grated cheese, walnuts and herbs into the flour mixture then add the blended yeast and enough water to make a smooth, slightly sticky dough. Knead the dough until smooth and stretchy. Place in the mixing bowl and cover either with a damp tea-towel or oiled cling film.

Stand the bowl on a trivet on top of the Aga and leave to rise until doubled in size.

Turn the dough onto a lightly floured work surface and knock back lightly. Shape the dough into a loaf and place in the prepared tin. For the topping, scatter the cheese over the loaf. Re-cover with the tea-towel and leave to rise again on the Aga until the bread has just risen above the lip of the tin.

Put the shelf on the floor of the roasting oven and bake for 35-40 minutes. Check the loaf after 20 minutes and if the cheese is browning too much, slide in the cold shelf on the second set of runners from the top and bake for an additional 5 minutes.

To test if cooked, tap the bottom of the loaf; if it sounds hollow it is baked. Turn out and cool on a wire rack.

RAISIN BREAD FOR CHEESE

I like the combination of fruit and cheese for lunch and this fruit loaf makes a great alternative to the usual bread and cheese. I've used Lexia raisins because they are very plump and moist but any type will do. If the raisins you have are a little dry, just soak them in warm water for half an hour before use.

350g/12oz wholemeal flour
350g/12oz strong white flour
2 teaspoons salt
15g/1/2oz yeast
1 tablespoon treacle
150g/5oz Lexia raisins
425ml/3/4 pint water

Place the flours and the salt in a mixing bowl and stir in the raisins. In a basin, blend the yeast, treacle and a little water together. Add to the flours along with the remaining water. Mix to a dough, ensuring no flour is left at the bottom of the bowl. Knead the dough for 10 minutes. Place in an oiled mixing bowl, cover with either a damp tea-towel or oiled cling film and put to rise on the Aga until doubled in size.

Tip the dough out onto a lightly floured worktop and gently knock back. Cut the dough in half, and shape each half into an oblong loaf. Place on a lightly greased and floured baking tray or one lined with Bake-O-Glide. Cover with oiled cling film or a damp tea-towel. Place on top of the Aga and allow the loaves to rise until doubled in size.

Hang the tin on the bottom set of runners of the roasting oven and bake for 25-30 minutes, until golden brown and sounding hollow when tapped on the bottom. Cool on a wire rack.

Makes 2 loaves

BARA BRITH

This is classic Welsh fruited bread; similar ones are made at Selkirk Bannock and Barm Brack in Ireland. As I do a lot of Aga cookery demonstrations in Wales I have chosen the Welsh option!

450g/1lb strong white flour
1 teaspoon salt
1 level teaspoon mixed spice
75g/3oz butter
75g/3 oz Demerara sugar
450g/1lb mixed dried fruit
1 egg, beaten
25g/1oz yeast
200ml/7fl oz milk

Measure the flour, salt and mixed spice in a mixing bowl. Add the butter and rub in until the mixture resembles breadcrumbs. Stir in the sugar and the dried fruit. In a separate bowl, blend the yeast with a little milk to make a paste. Add the yeast to the flour mixture and then add the beaten egg and the remaining milk. Mix all the ingredients together to make dough. Knead the dough until smooth and stretchy. Put the dough into a bowl and cover with oiled cling film. Stand on a trivet on top of the Aga and leave to rise until doubled in size.

Grease and flour 2 x ½kg (1lb) loaf tins.

Turn the risen dough out onto a lightly floured worktop and gently knock back. Cut the dough into two even portions and shape each into a loaf. Place the loaves in the prepared tins. Cover with oiled cling film and stand on a trivet on top of the Aga until the dough has risen to the rim of the tin. To bake, put the shelf on the floor of the roasting oven, slide in the tins and bake the Bara Brith for 30-35 minutes, until golden brown and sounding hollow when tapped. Turn onto a wire rack to cool.

Makes 2 loaves

MALT LOAF

This sticky loaf, that keeps so well, is one of my son Dominic's favourites. Serve sliced and buttered. When buying malt extract from your chemist, make sure that you don't buy one with cod liver oil added, as the flavour will be quite wrong!

4 tablespoons malt extract
2 tablespoons black treacle
25g/1oz butter
450g/1lb strong plain flour
1 teaspoon salt
225g/8oz sultanas
25g/1oz yeast
175ml/6fl oz water
2 tablespoons honey warmed on the back
of the Aga, for the glaze

Put the malt extract, black treacle and the butter into a basin and stand at the back of the Aga until the butter has melted. Stir together.

Measure the flour, salt and sultanas into a mixing bowl. In a basin, blend the yeast with some of the water. Add the malt extract mixture to the flour along with the yeast and most of the water. Mix to a slightly sticky dough, adding more water as needed. Knead the dough until smooth and elastic. Place the dough in a lightly greased bowl and cover with either a damp tea-towel or oiled cling film. Stand on a trivet on top of the Aga until doubled in size.

Grease and flour 2 x ½kg (1lb) loaf tins.

Turn the risen dough out onto a lightly floured worktop and cut the dough in half. Shape each half into a loaf and place in the tins. Stand on a trivet on top of the Aga and cover with oiled cling film. Leave to rise until the loaf has risen to the rim of the tin. This is a heavy mixture so it may take some time.

Put the shelf on the floor of the roasting oven. Remove the cling film and put in the loaves. Bake for 35-40 minutes, until golden brown and sounding hollow when tapped. Turn onto a wire rack and glaze with runny honey.

Makes 2 loaves

CHELSEA BUNS

These buns remind me of my teacher training days in the 70's, when it was this recipe that was thought perfect for teaching basic skills.

450g/1lb strong plain flour
1 teaspoon salt
50g/2oz caster sugar
15g/¹/₂oz yeast
225 ml/8fl oz lukewarm milk
1 egg, beaten
50g /2oz butter, melted

For the filling
75g/3oz soft brown sugar
175g/6oz mixed dried fruit
50g/2oz butter melted

For the glaze
2 tablespoons caster sugar
3 tablespoons milk

Measure the flour, salt and sugar into a mixing bowl. In a separate bowl, blend the yeast together with a little milk and add to the flour mixture. Then add the egg, melted butter and the remaining milk. Mix to a dough and then knead until smooth and stretchy. Place in a bowl and cover with a damp tea-towel or oiled cling film. Stand on a trivet on top of the Aga and leave to rise until doubled in volume.

Grease and line the base of a 23cm (9 inch) square cake tin. Turn the dough out onto a lightly floured worktop. Knock back lightly and then roll to a rectangle, roughly 40 x 22.5cm (16 x 9 inches). In a bowl, mix the filling ingredients together and then spread these evenly over the rolled out dough. Roll the dough tightly, from the longest side, like a Swiss roll. Using a sharp knife cut into 9 even portions. Lay the portions in the prepared tin, cut side uppermost. Cover with oiled cling film and return to the top of the Aga. Allow to rise until the dough fills the tin.

To bake, put the oven shelf on the floor of the roasting oven and slide in the tin of buns. Bake for 25-30 minutes, until the buns are golden brown and slide from the tin easily.

Prepare the glaze: heat the milk and sugar gently on the simmering plate until the sugar has dissolved. Bring to the boil and bubble well for 1 minute. As soon as the buns come out of the oven, brush them with the glaze. Cool on a wire rack.

Makes 9 buns

HOT CROSS BUNS

These days, of course, hot cross buns are available in the shops from New Year onwards. But I find that baking them in your Aga on Good Friday always makes them a special treat.

200g/2lbs strong white flour
1 teaspoon salt
3-4 teaspoons mixed spice, depending on taste
110g/4oz caster sugar
250g/8oz sultanas or currants or mixed peel
25g/1oz fresh yeast
430ml/15fl oz milk and water, mixed
110g/4oz butter
2 eggs, beaten

For the crosses
4 tablespoons plain flour

For the sticky glaze
4 tablespoons caster sugar
4 tablespoons milk

Place the flour, salt, mixed spice and sugar in a mixing bowl. Add the butter and rub into the dry ingredients. In a separate bowl, blend the yeast with a little milk. Add the dried fruit and yeast mixture to the dry ingredients. Add the beaten eggs and most of the milk. Mix the dough, adding more milk as needed, to make the dough smooth and just slightly sticky. Knead the dough for 5 minutes. Place in a large lightly oiled mixing bowl, and cover with oiled cling film. Place on or near the Aga, until risen to twice its original size.

Grease and flour two large baking trays.

Turn the dough out onto a floured worktop and knock back gently. Divide the dough into 24 even portions. Shape each portion into a roll. Onto each baking tray place 12 buns, allowing space for the buns to spread. Cover with oiled cling film or a damp tea-towel.

Allow to rise until doubled in size.

To make the paste for the crosses, put 4 tablespoons of flour in a basin and blend with cold water to make a paste about the consistency of double cream. Put this paste into a plastic food bag and tie it closed. Snip a tiny corner off the base of the bag and pipe crosses onto the buns.

I find it best to bake one tray at a time, so put one tray on a cooler worktop if the buns are risen. Alternatively, leave to rise further.

Hang the baking tray on the bottom set of runners of the roasting oven and bake for 20 minutes; after 10 minutes check the buns to see they are not over browning, if they are, cover them with foil, and continue to bake until they are golden brown and sounding hollow when tapped. Move to a cooling rack and brush on the glaze.

To prepare the glaze, place the milk and sugar in a saucepan and stand on the simmering plate. Stir to dissolve the sugar and then bubble for 2-3 minutes. Brush the hot glaze onto the buns as soon as they come out of the oven. This will give a lovely sticky bun. Cool on a wire rack. Bake and glaze the remaining buns in the same way. These can be made in advance and frozen. Thaw at room temperature and refresh in the simmering oven.

Makes 24 hot cross buns

CHOCOLATE LOAF

I often used to buy delicious chocolate bread from my local supermarket to have as a special treat on Sunday morning. Sadly, it's no longer available so this is my attempt to mimic that loaf – tasty but not always perfect!

450g/1lb strong white flour
1 teaspoon salt
50g/2oz caster sugar
15g/1/2oz yeast
300ml/1/2 pint milk and water mixed
2 eggs, beaten
50g/2oz butter, melted
2 tablespoons chocolate spread

For the glaze
beaten egg

Mix the flour, salt and sugar together in a mixing bowl. Blend the yeast with a little of the milk and water mixture. Add the yeast to the flour with the eggs and melted butter. Mix together, adding more liquid as needed, to make a smooth and pliable dough. Knead well until the dough is stretchy. Place in a greased bowl and cover either with a damp tea-towel or oiled cling film and stand on a trivet on top of the Aga to rise until doubled in volume.

Grease and flour a 1/2kg (1lb) loaf tin.

Turn the dough onto a lightly floured worktop and roll out to an oblong shape, roughly 30.5 x 20.5cm (12 x 8 inches). Spread the chocolate over the dough right to the edges. Roll up tightly, as you would a Swiss roll. Cut the roll into 4 even portions. Place the four pieces of dough randomly but touching each other in the tin. Cover with oiled cling film or a damp tea-towel and stand on a trivet on the Aga to rise until reaching just above the rim of the tin. Gently glaze the top of the loaf.

Place the shelf on the floor of the roasting oven, slide in the loaf and bake for 30-35 minutes. If after 20 minutes the loaf is browning too much, slide the cold shelf onto the second set of runners from the top of the oven. Cook until the loaf is golden brown and sounding hollow when tapped. Cool on a wire rack.

Makes 1 loaf

TEACAKES FOR TOASTING

These are always popular in our house for Sunday tea. I find that it is useful to keep a batch in the freezer; simply split the teacakes before freezing so that they can then be quickly thawed and toasted directly on the simmering plate.

450g/1lb strong white flour
1 teaspoon salt
15g/¹/₂oz yeast
300ml/¹/₂ pint milk
25g/1oz caster sugar
50g/2oz butter, melted
50g/2oz currants

Measure the flour and salt into a mixing bowl. In a separate bowl, mix the yeast together with some of the milk to make a paste and add this to the flour along with the caster sugar, butter and the currants. Mix to a dough, adding more milk as necessary, to make a smooth and pliable dough. Knead the dough until smooth and stretchy. Return to the bowl and cover with a damp tea-towel or oiled cling film. Stand the bowl on a trivet on top of the Aga until the dough has doubled in size. Grease and flour a large baking tray or line it with Bake-O-Glide.

Turn the risen dough out onto a lightly floured worktop. Knock back the dough and then divide into 8 even portions. Form each portion into a smooth-topped roll and place on the prepared baking tray. When all the teacakes have been shaped, flatten the rolls with the palm of your hands. Brush the tops with a little milk and return the tin to the top of the Aga. Leave to rise until almost doubled in size. Brush again with milk. Hang the baking tray on the bottom set of runners of the roasting oven and bake for 20-25 minutes, until golden brown and sounding hollow when tapped. Cool on a wire rack. To serve, split open and butter, or toast with the cut side down on the simmering plate until golden brown.

Makes 8 teacakes

CAKES

INTRODUCTION

I have to admit that I am essentially a lazy cook. I like to find the quickest way of ending up with a brilliant finished dish. I was taught and trained in the traditional cake-making methods, but these days, with the help of ingredients such as whipped margarine and butters, and chopped, washed fruits, cake-making has never been easier. I would rather have a good, wholesome and tasty cake made quickly at home than a commercially made one able to be kept for weeks! So if you normally make cakes by the traditional 'creaming' method, then have a go at the 'quick method' Victoria sandwich (*see page 84*) and see what the results are like!

FLOUR

Standard cake-making flour is soft flour (as opposed to strong flour for breads). It is the standard, everyday plain or self-raising flour sold in grocers and supermarkets. As with all ingredients, buy fresh from a shop that has a fast turnover. If you keep your flour in a container rather than the bag, then do not add new flour onto old flour. Periodically wash out the container to keep weevils at bay. If you don't do a lot of baking, then plain flour and baking powder can be used as opposed to self-raising. Either way, I rarely bother to sieve flour these days as most flours are well sieved before they are sold. The only time I would sieve is if the recipe demands that the ingredients be very well blended. Cheaper flours may not have been milled as finely or sieved so much as the more expensive flours, but will certainly make good cakes. Try a range of flours and see which one you get on best with.

SUGAR

The standard sugar used for cakes is caster sugar. This is a fine sugar that mixes in easily. It can sometimes be substituted with soft brown sugar, which although fine has more moisture and of course colour. Demerara sugar and granulated sugar have large crystals and add crunch to the texture of the cake; they are often used in toppings. Icing sugar has a fine, powder like texture, used in icing or toppings. Most of these sugars are now available unrefined, are are slightly brown, but have more flavour.

When weighing sugar be careful not to 'over weigh' as this can give a crisp texture to the cake.

BUTTER

There is no doubt that real butter will impart the best flavour in cooking and is the only fat to use for some things, like shortbread. Butter needs to be at room temperature for any 'creaming' methods; just keep the butter on the side in the kitchen. I would only use it straight from the fridge for 'rubbing-in'. Choose unsalted butter whenever possible.

MARGARINE AND BUTTER/OIL BLENDS

Being realistic, many of us bake with whipped fats. They are easy to use straight from the fridge and are cheaper than butter. For most baking they will give you excellent results. In fact, 'all-in-one method cakes' must be made with whipped fats for the best results. I will indicate where butter or hard fats are essential within the recipes in this book. Don't be tempted to use 'low-fat' varieties, as these contain water and do not give a good result.

EGGS

All the recipes have been tested using 'large' eggs. For baking, they need to be kept at room temperature. I always buy free-range hens eggs, however that's just my personal choice.

DRIED FRUITS

Most dried fruits come ready-washed these days, though I still seem to find some currants gritty. Sometimes the fruit is stuck together in the packet, so spend a minute breaking it up. Glacé fruits, like cherries, need washing and some fruits may need soaking, such as apricots. I find that chopping these fruits is sometimes easiest done with a pair of scissors.

CHOCOLATE

Unless specified, I use a dark cooking chocolate, for most cakes about 52% is fine or for something richer 70%. For cocoa, I have a preference for Green and Blacks organic cocoa. This is because I find it gives the best depth of flavour.

Spices and raising agents are measured in level teaspoons. It's worth buying a set of measuring spoons if you do a lot of baking, but don't be overly concerned about absolute accuracy. My mother was a brilliant cook and measured many things by eye or the handful. Once you have been cooking a while you will begin to get the 'feel' for what you are doing.

EQUIPMENT

If you like cooking and do a reasonable amount then it is always worth buying good quality equipment. It's easier to use and lasts longer.

I have a **Kitchen Aid mixer** that's heavily used for bread making and sometimes used for cake making. I use it for creaming butter and sugar and adding the eggs for rich fruit cakes. When I add dried fruit to a mixture in the mixer, then I always do this at the end of mixing to avoid the fruit becoming squashed. I also whisk egg whites with the Kitchen Aid, which works brilliantly.

I sometimes use my **Magimix processor** for cakes, but I prefer the standard mixer. However, it is excellent for chopping fruits and making crumble toppings.

Warning! Cakes made using 'the all-in-one-method' of mixing can end up being over mixed; so if you want to use the mixer, resist the temptation to give a thorough, high speed mix before spooning into the tin!

You will need a selection of **bowls** and **basins**, any you prefer. **Measuring jugs** are essential and one **sieve** for occasional flour sieving and for icing sugar. **Measuring spoons** are useful if you like to bake a lot. A **lemon squeezer** that strains the pips is useful. A **Microplane grater**, though expensive, is brilliant for grating ingredients such as nutmegs, citrus rinds.

The Aga comes with large and small **roasting tins** that are excellent for tray-bakes of different sizes. You can also buy **baking trays** from your Aga supplier that fit on the runners; these come in the same sizes as the roasting tins and are an excellent buy. I make all my Swiss rolls and roulades in these tins.

The Aga shops also sell a very good range of bakeware and, although many people think it expensive, it will last a lifetime. It is non-stick and enamelled and won't have a chance of rusting if you dry it on the Aga! Lightly grease the sides and base-line with **Bake-O-Glide** and your cakes will easily slide onto the cooling rack. Most of the recipes have been tested in these tins. I line all my tins with Bake-O-Glide. This wonderful re-usable, non-stick flexible sheet saves hours of lining tins and gives you the confidence that nothing will stick.

The **Cold Shelf** or **Plain Shelf** is a very important piece of equipment for a two-oven Aga owner, used for reducing the heat in the hot oven, especially for cake baking. The cold shelf should be kept out of the oven, somewhere cool for when you need it. The cold shelf is put two runners above the top of the cake tin, thus allowing the cake to rise and the hot air to circulate. The cold shelf remains effective at keeping the temperature below it lower than normal for about 40 minutes. If you are doing a lot of baking, you may need to cool the shelf down between batches or have two cold shelves to alternate.

A Few Tips on Making and Baking Rich Fruit Cakes

Rich fruit cakes baked in the Aga are the best you will ever eat!

You only need to line the base of the tins and not the sides. I butter the sides but don't bother with lining the sides. Forget wrapping paper round the outside of the tin: it is unnecessary.

Most fruits are sold washed these days, but I do try to give currants a dust with flour through a sieve to remove some of their grittiness. Cherries need to be rinsed of their sugar syrup, otherwise they will be too heavy and sink. Only use butter to make rich fruit cakes, not only is the flavour better but the finished cake will not be so crumbly. Have eggs at room temperature to prevent curdling.

If you level the mixture in the tin, the cake will come out with a level top (easy for decorating!). Rich fruit cakes are best cooked from cold in the simmering oven. If you haven't made a cake in your Aga before, I recommend that you bake the cake during the day and keep an eye on it. Make a note on the recipe page of how long it has taken to bake. 12-plus hours is not unusual. The cake is cooked when it looks dry on the top, has shrunk from the sides of the tin and a skewer inserted into the middle comes out clean.

Cool all cakes in the tin. When the cake is cold it can be wrapped in foil and stored in an airtight tin. If you like to 'feed' your cake before decorating, prick the top with a skewer and spoon over two or three tablespoons of brandy. Re-wrap. Do this two or three times.

THE CAKE BAKER

Many people ask me about the Cake Baker. If you have a three- or four-oven Aga you do not need a Cake Baker. If you have a two-oven Aga and are only making a deep cake such as a Madeira or a Dundee once a year, then it is an expensive investment. However, if you make a lot of cakes there is no doubt that a Cake Baker gives excellent results.

A small explanation: the roasting oven is too hot to bake a deep cake through to the middle without burning the outside. To overcome this, the Cake Baker was introduced in 1967. To use, put the shelf on the floor of the roasting oven. The outer or stock pot is put into the roasting oven to heat through while the cake is being prepared. Remember to remove the trivet and the cake tins first, otherwise they are too hot to handle! Prepare the cake and put it in one of the tins. Fix the tin into the trivet. Remove the Cake Baker from the oven, drop in the cake in the trivet, replace the lid and return the Cake Baker to the oven. I find most cakes bake in $1^1/_4$-$1^1/_2$ hours. Test and cool in the usual way.

Problems arise when trying to bake square or loaf tin cakes, as the Cake Baker only comes as a round shape. The method I have found most effective to deal with square and loaf tin cakes is as follows. Stand the cake tin in the large roasting tin. Cover loosely with foil and slide the tin onto the bottom set of runners of the roasting oven. Put the cold shelf onto the third set of runners from the bottom. Most cakes should be cooked in 45-50 minutes with this method. I have also put a tin inside an old biscuit tin; this works quite well for the smaller cakes, but do keep an eye on them!

VICTORIA SANDWICH

Victoria Sandwich is traditionally made by the 'creaming method'. This means that the butter and sugar are beaten or 'creamed' together until light and fluffy. The arrival on the market of whipped, soft tub margarines meant that we could all make simple sponge cakes by the 'all-in-one' method. I find that I get the best results using this quick and easy method. These types of margarine, or whipped buttermilk and oil, make excellent cakes and can be used straight from the fridge, however, the results will be better if you use them at room temperature.

TRADITIONAL VICTORIA SANDWICH

This easy-to-make cake will be spongy and moist. Be very accurate with the sugar, as over-weighing will cause the cake to be crusty and shiny on top.

3 eggs
175g/6oz self-raising flour
175g/6oz soft tub margarine
175g/6oz caster sugar
1 teaspoon vanilla essence

For the filling
2-3 tablespoons raspberry jam

For the topping
1 tablespoon caster sugar

Grease and line the base of 2 x 20cm (8 inch) Victoria Sandwich tins. Place the eggs, flour, margarine, caster sugar and vanilla essence in a mixing bowl. Stir well with a wooden spoon until light and fluffy and all the margarine has been mixed in. Divide the mixture evenly between the two prepared tins.

For the two-oven Aga, put the shelf on the floor of the roasting oven. Put the cake tins on the shelf (I put mine to the right of the oven to avoid any 'hot spots'). Slide the cold shelf onto the second set of runners from the bottom. Bake for 25-30 minutes until the cake is risen, golden brown and firm to the touch when lightly pressed in the middle.

For the three- and four-oven Agas, hang the shelf on the bottom set of runners of the baking oven. Slide in the cakes and bake for 30-35 minutes, until risen, golden brown and firm to the touch when lightly pressed in the middle.

Turn the cakes gently out onto a cooling rack until cold. Place one cake upside down on a serving plate. Spread over the jam and place the second cake on top. Dust with icing sugar.

Makes 2 cakes

Flavours and Fillings

The basic Victoria Sandwich mixture can be flavoured with any of the following. Simply substitute these for the vanilla essence. **Lemon**: add the finely grated rind and juice of 1 lemon. **Coffee**: add 2 teaspoons of Camp coffee essence or 2 teaspoons of instant coffee blended with a drop of hot water. **Coffee and walnut**: add 2 teaspoons of coffee essence and 50g (2oz) of chopped walnuts. **Chocolate**: blend 1 tablespoon of cocoa powder with 2 tablespoons of hot water.

Raspberry is the traditional jam filling of choice, but you should experiment with other flavours. Adding a little whipped double cream is lovely (but wait until the cake is completely cold). I like to add lemon or orange curd – further adding a little cream is a quick way to something special! And for a speedy chocolate cake, I use chocolate spread as a filling. See overleaf for **Butter Icing**.

BUTTER ICING

Butter icing can be flavoured with coffee, vanilla or chocolate. To fill and top the cake you will need:

110g/4oz margarine
225g/8oz icing sugar
2 tablespoons milk

Flavour with any one of the following
1 teaspoon vanilla essence,
2 teaspoons coffee essence,
1 tablespoon cocoa powder (sieved with the icing sugar), grated rind and juice of 1 lemon or orange

Place the margarine, icing sugar, milk and your flavouring of choice in a bowl, and stir with a wooden spoon until light and fluffy.

TRAY BAKES

I have noticed over recent years that oblong cakes baked in a roasting tin get eaten more quickly than round cakes. I still haven't worked out why! So now I often make a tray bake, topped with icing and cut into squares. Below are a few favourites. Base all recipes on the 3-egg Victoria Sandwich recipe (see p84). Add your choice of flavouring.

Line the small roasting tin with a sheet of Bake-O-Glide and spoon in the cake mixture.

For a two-oven Aga, hang the tin on the bottom set of runners of the roasting oven. Slide the cold shelf onto the second set of runners from the top of the oven and bake the cake for 25-30 minutes, until golden brown and firm to the touch when pressed lightly in the middle. For the three- and four-oven Aga, hang the tin on the bottom set of runners of the baking oven and bake the cake for 30-35 minutes, until golden brown and firm to the touch when lightly pressed in the middle.

FLAVOURS AND FILLINGS

Sultana: add 110g (4oz) of sultanas to the sponge mixture and stir. Dust with caster sugar to serve. **Apple**: chop 2 peeled and cored apples into the sponge mixture. Lay apple slices over the top of the sponge before baking. **Chocolate chips**: add 100g (3½oz) packet chocolate chips to the cake mix. See overleaf for **Coffee with Fudge Frosting**.

COFFEE WITH FUDGE FROSTING

Add 1 tablespoon of coffee essence to the Tray Bake cake mix and then ice with coffee fudge frosting:

50g/2oz butter
110g/4oz soft brown sugar
3 tablespoons coffee essence
1 tablespoon single cream
225g/8oz icing sugar

Place the butter, soft brown sugar, coffee essence and cream in a saucepan. Heat gently, stirring, until the butter has melted and the sugar dissolved. Bring to the boil and boil for 2-3 minutes. Remove from the heat and gradually stir in the icing sugar. Beat until smooth, and when cool spread onto the cake.

SWISS ROLL

A Swiss roll is a great stand-by cake, quickly made and baked in 8 minutes. I find that when made in the Aga, Swiss rolls remain moist, with no crusty edge to trim (so no cook's perks!). The roll will keep for a couple of days.

2 eggs
50g/2oz caster sugar
50g/2oz self-raising flour
2 tablespoons raspberry jam
2 teaspoons caster sugar

Line the small baking tray with a sheet of Bake-O-Glide.

Place the eggs and caster sugar in a bowl and whisk until thick, pale and creamy. The mixture should leave a trail when a little is dribbled over the top. Gently scatter the flour over the surface of the egg mixture and fold in gently but thoroughly - I find a plastic spatula is best for this.

Carefully pour the mixture into the prepared tray. Hang the tray on the bottom set of runners of the roasting oven and bake for 8 minutes, until evenly golden brown and firm to the touch when lightly pressed.

Place a plain sheet of Bake-O-Glide on a work surface and scatter with the caster sugar. Tip the cooked Swiss roll out onto the Bake-O-Glide and peel off the lining sheet. Spread over the jam and tightly roll from the end. It should be pliable enough to tuck in well. Then continue rolling. Cool on a wire rack.

You can make a larger Swiss roll by using the large baking tray and a 5-egg mixture. If you would like cream in the filling, just wait until the cake is cold and then gently un-roll. Spread with whipped cream and then re-roll.

LEMON BUTTER POUND CAKE

This is a Madeira cake, but called a Pound cake because the flour, butter, caster sugar and eggs all weigh the same. If you have a two-oven Aga and own a Cake Baker then use it for this recipe (see p83 for instructions).

175g/6oz plain flour
2 level teaspoons baking powder
pinch salt
175g/6oz butter, softened
175g/6oz caster sugar
3 eggs, beaten
grated rind and juice 1 lemon

For the lemon butter icing
110g/4oz butter, softened
350g/12oz icing sugar
grated rind and juice 1 lemon
star fruit slices or physalis to decorate

Grease and line the base of a 20cm (8 inch) deep cake tin.

Mix the flour, baking power and salt together on a plate. Put the butter and sugar together in a mixing bowl and beat together. Beat in the eggs and then fold in the flour and the rind and juice of the lemon. Spoon the mixture into the prepared tin.

If using a Cake Baker, bake for 40-45 minutes.

For a two-oven Aga put the shelf on the floor of the roasting oven. Put in the cake and slide the cold shelf onto the second set of runners from the top of the roasting oven. Bake the cake for 35-40 minutes, until risen, firm to the touch and slightly shrunk from the sides of the tin.

For a three- or four-oven Aga put the shelf on the bottom set of runners of the baking oven. Put in the cake and bake for 40-45 minutes, until risen, firm to the touch and slightly shrunk from the sides of the tin.

Leave in the tin for 10 minutes and then turn onto a wire rack to cool completely.

To make the icing, beat the butter until creamy and then add the icing sugar, a spoonful at a time. When you have incorporated all of the icing sugar, beat in the lemon rind.

Cut the cake in half horizontally and sandwich together with the icing. Place on a serving plate. Spread the remaining icing over the top and sides and decorate with the fruit before cutting.

MADEIRA CAKE

Many people think this cake must contain Madeira, but actually it was originally made as an accompaniment to the wine. Its firm but light texture is ideal for supporting a heavy icing, such as on a Christening cake. For best results cook, in the Cake Baker or the baking oven. If you are using the roasting oven, do watch that it doesn't get over cooked on the sides. If that begins to happen, change the roasting tin or put a cold baking tray underneath the cake after 40 minutes.

175g/6oz softened butter of margarine
175g/6oz caster sugar
1 teaspoon vanilla essence
3 eggs
110g/4oz plain flour
110g/4oz self-raising flour
1-2 tablespoons milk
2-3 thin slices citron peel

Grease and line the base of an 18cm (7 inch) deep round cake tin.

Place the butter, sugar, vanilla essence, eggs and flours in a mixing bowl and stir until evenly mixed and light. Add a little milk, if needed, to give a dropping consistency. Spoon the mixture into the prepared tin.

For the two-oven Aga, bake in the pre-heated Cake Baker for 1 hour, or put the tin in the large roasting tin and cover loosely with foil and hang the tin on the second set of runners from the bottom of the roasting oven. Slide the cold shelf onto the second set of runners from the top of the oven and bake for 30 minutes. Pull out the cake and lay the citron peel on the top of the cake. Return to the oven and bake for a further 20-30 minutes, until the cake is risen, golden brown and a skewer inserted in the middle comes out clean.

For the three- and four-oven Aga, hang the oven shelf on the bottom set of runners of the baking oven. Put in the cake and bake for 30 minutes. Pull the cake out and lay the citron peel on top of the cake. Return the cake and bake for a further 30-40 minutes, until the cake is golden brown and a skewer inserted in the middle comes out clean.

Cool the cake for 10 minutes in the tin and then turn onto a wire rack to cool.

MARBLE CAKE

Marble cakes always look impressive but are actually simple to make. This is a slightly more sophisticated version of my 'Swirly Chocolate Tray Bake', from *The Traditional Aga Cookery Book*.

110g/4oz plain dark chocolate, melted
125ml/4 fl oz milk
110g/4oz softened butter or tub margarine
175g/6oz caster sugar
2 eggs
225g/8oz self-raising flour
1 teaspoon baking powder
3 tablespoons plain, thick yoghurt or soured cream

Grease and line the base of a ¹/₂kg (1lb) loaf tin.

Mix half the milk into the melted chocolate and blend well. You may need to warm it through.

In a mixing bowl, place the butter, sugar, eggs, self-raising flour, baking powder and the yoghurt or soured cream. Mix well until the mixture is smooth and light. Divide the mixture evenly between two bowls. Stir the chocolate into one mixture and the remaining milk into the other mixture. Place spoonfuls of mixture in the prepared loaf tin, alternating between the chocolate and plain mixture. Pass a table knife once through the mixture to marble the ingredients.

For the two-oven Aga, place the shelf on the floor of the roasting oven. Slide in the cake and hang the cold shelf on the second set of runners from the top of the oven. Bake for 40-45 minutes.

For the three- or four-oven Aga, hang the shelf on the bottom set of runners of the baking oven. Bake for 50-55 minutes.

The cake will be firm when lightly pressed and a skewer inserted in the middle comes out clean. Cool for 10 minutes in the tin and then turn out onto a wire rack to cool.

ALMOND CAKE

I love this light but moist cake – it's perfect served either on its own or with fruit, and is nearly as good accompanied with a cup of tea as with a glass of good dessert wine! It really is worth making the effort to grind the nuts yourself rather than using ready-ground almonds – the texture is far superior.

300g/10 oz blanched almonds
300g/10oz caster sugar
8 egg whites
grated rind 1 lemon
75g/3oz plain flour

Butter and line the base of a 22cm (9 inch) spring-release cake tin.

Place the almonds and the caster sugar into a food processor and grind the nuts fairly finely.

In a clean bowl, whisk the egg whites until stiff. Fold in the almond mixture and then add the lemon rind. Sieve the flour over the mixture and fold in. Place the mixture in the prepared tin. Smooth off the top.

For a two-oven Aga, place the shelf on the floor of the roasting oven. Slide in the cake tin and put the cold shelf on the third set of runners from the top of the oven. Bake for 20 minutes and then transfer to the simmering oven for about one hour, or until a skewer comes clean from the centre of the cake.

For a three- or four-oven Aga, place the shelf on the bottom set of runners of the baking oven and bake for one hour or until a skewer comes clean from the centre of the cake.

Cool in the tin, remove the side and then leave on a wire rack until cold.

MAYPOLE CAKE

I originally made this cake for a May Day cookery demonstration in the Bath Aga shop. The decorations remind me of a wonderful birthday cake my mother once made for me.

3 eggs
175g/6oz self-raising flour
175g/6oz caster sugar
175g/6oz soft margarine
1 teaspoon vanilla essence
2 tablespoons apricot jam

For the frosting
1 egg white
3 tablespoons hot water
200g/7oz caster sugar
2 pinches cream of tartar
1/2 teaspoon vanilla essence

To decorate
1 meat skewer
ribbons in a variety of colours

Grease and line the base with Bake-O-Glide, 2 x 20.5cm (8 inch) Victoria Sandwich tins.

Measure the eggs, flour, caster sugar, margarine and vanilla essence into a mixing bowl. Beat together using a wooden spoon, until the mixture is smooth, taking care not to over-mix. Divide the mixture between the two prepared tins and smooth the top.

For a two-oven Aga, put the shelf on the floor of the roasting oven. Put the prepared cakes in and slide the cold shelf onto the second set of runners from the bottom of the oven. Bake for 20-25 minutes until risen, golden brown and firm to the touch when lightly pressed in the middle.

For a three- or four-oven Aga, hang the shelf on the bottom set of runners of the baking oven. Put in the cakes and bake for 25-30 minutes until risen, golden brown and firm to the touch when lightly pressed in the middle.

Turn the cakes out onto a cooling rack until cold.

To decorate, place one cake upside down on a serving plate and spread with the apricot jam. Place the second cake, the right way up, on top.

To prepare the frosting, place the egg white, water, caster sugar and cream of tartar in the bowl of an electric mixer and whisk until the mixture has become white and frothy. Whisk in the vanilla essence. Cover the cake with the frosting and roughen slightly all over.

Fix the ribbons to the meat skewer either with glue or thumb tack. Insert the skewer through the middle of the cake and then lay out the ribbons round the cake.

Cuts into 8-10 slices

FLOURLESS CHOCOLATE CAKE

This is a perfect recipe for anyone on a wheat-free diet. But whatever sort of diet you are on, it makes a delicious cake and can be served with fruit for a dessert.

200g/7oz plain chocolate
150g/5oz butter
175g/6oz caster sugar
175g/6oz ground almonds
5 eggs, separated

Grease and line the base of a 22cm (9 inch) spring-release cake tin.

Place the chocolate and butter in a basin and stand it at the back of the Aga until melted. Put the sugar and the ground almonds in a mixing bowl and add the egg yolks. Pour over the melted chocolate and butter and stir in.

Place the egg whites in a bowl and whisk until white and fluffy. Beat one tablespoon of the egg white into the chocolate mixture. Fold in the remaining egg whites. The mixture will be quite stiff, so you will need to be fairly firm during the folding in. Spoon the mixture into the prepared tin.

For the two-oven Aga, stand the shelf on the floor of the roasting oven. Slide in the cake tin and put the cold shelf on the second set of runners from the bottom of the oven. Bake for 40-45 minutes.

For the three- and four-oven Aga, put the shelf on the bottom set of runners of the baking oven and slide in the cake. Bake for 1 hour.

When the cake is cooked it will be firm to the touch and a skewer inserted in the middle will come out clean. Leave for 5 minutes in the tin and then remove and cool on a wire rack. Dust with icing sugar.

RED-VELVET CAKE

This wonderfully seductive cake is one I made for a Valentine's Day cookery demonstration. It looks stunning but is actually no more than a chocolate cake with a lot of red food colouring!

250g/9oz plain flour
1 scant teaspoon salt
50g/2oz cocoa powder
350g/12oz caster sugar
300ml/10fl oz corn oil
2 eggs
4 tablespoons red food colouring
1 teaspoon vanilla extract
225ml/8 fl oz buttermilk
1$^1/_2$ teaspoons bicarbonate of soda
2 teaspoons white wine vinegar

Grease and line the base of 2 x 23cm (9 inch) Victoria Sandwich tins.

Measure the flour, salt and cocoa powder into a bowl.

In a separate bowl, place the sugar and oil and beat until well combined. Add the eggs and beat well, then beat in the food colouring and vanilla essence. Fold in the flour and the buttermilk. Mix the bicarbonate of soda in a small basin with the vinegar and add to the batter and beat in well.

Divide the batter evenly between the prepared tins.

For the two-oven Aga, stand the shelf on the floor of the roasting oven and put in the cakes. Slide the cold shelf onto the second set of runners from the bottom. Bake the cakes for 25-30 minutes, until risen and firm to the touch.

For a three- or four-oven Aga, hang the shelf on the bottom set of runners of the baking oven. Slide in the cakes and bake for 35-40 minutes, until risen and firm to the touch.

Cool in the tins for 5 minutes and then turn out onto a cooling rack. Cool completely before icing.

Repeat the frosting method as for the Maypole Cake recipe (see p96). Use some of the frosting to sandwich the cakes together. Place on a serving plate and then spread the remaining frosting over the top and sides of the cake. Swirl with a knife.

This cake is best eaten within 6 hours of frosting.

FISHGUARD GINGERBREAD

I did some research for a St David's Day cookery demonstration in the Cardiff Aga shop and uncovered this traditional recipe – it has since become one of my favourites.

110g/4oz butter
75g/3oz soft brown sugar
1 egg, beaten
150g/5oz black treacle
350g/12oz self raising flour
1/2 teaspoon salt
1 teaspoon ground ginger
1/2 teaspoon bicarbonate soda
150ml/5fl oz buttermilk
150g/5oz sultanas or raisins

Line the small roasting tin with Bake-O-Glide.

Put the butter and soft brown sugar into a large bowl and beat until mixed. Beat in the egg and the treacle, adding a little flour to help the mixing in. In a separate bowl, sieve together the flour, salt, ground ginger and bicarbonate of soda and then fold this into the butter mixture. Stir in the buttermilk to slacken the mixture and finally fold in the sultanas or raisins.

Spoon the mixture into the prepared tin.

For the two-oven Aga, hang the tin on the bottom set of runners of the roasting oven and slide the cold shelf onto the third set of runners from the top. Bake the gingerbread for 35-40 minutes.

For the three- and four-oven Aga, hang the tin on the bottom set of runners of the baking oven for 35-40 minutes.

Bake until risen and firm to the touch and a skewer comes out clean. Cool in the tin for 10 minutes and then transfer to a wire rack until cold. Cut into squares.

CHERRY AND MARZIPAN CAKE

I discovered this recipe when an Aga customer came to me for advice. She was having difficulty getting the cake to cook in the middle. After several attempts, I discovered the best solution was to bake it in a loaf tin. I am sure it will become a favourite. So thank you, Melanie.

225g/8oz butter or margarine
225g/8oz caster sugar
4 eggs, beaten
225g/8oz self-raising flour
110g/4oz ground almonds
225g/8oz glacé cherries, halved and washed
½ teaspoon almond essence
250g/9oz marzipan

Grease and line the base of a 1kg (2lb) loaf tin.

Place the butter, sugar, eggs and flour in a bowl and mix until smooth. Stir in the glacé cherries and the almond essence. Spoon half the mixture into the prepared tin. Roll the marzipan to a strip just a little smaller than the length and width of the tin. Place the marzipan on top of the cake mix and then top with the remaining mixture and level off.

For the two-oven Aga, stand the tin in the large roasting tin. Cover the top loosely with a sheet of foil. Slide the tin onto the bottom set of runners and slide the cold shelf onto the second set of runners from the top. Bake for 50-55 minutes, until the cake has risen, is pale golden and a skewer inserted into the middle comes out clean.

For a three- or four-oven Aga, hang the shelf on the bottom set of runners of the baking oven. Put the cake in to bake for 1-1¼ hours, until risen, golden and a skewer inserted into the middle comes out clean.

Cool in the tin for 10 minutes and then turn out and cool on a wire rack. Dust with icing sugar.

BLUEBERRY CRUMB CAKE

Blueberries, loved by Americans, have become increasingly popular here and this version is adapted from a classic recipe. The richness of this cake is offset perfectly by the moist blueberries.

250g/9oz plain flour
1 level teaspoon baking powder
1 level teaspoon bicarbonate of soda
pinch salt
100g/3½ oz butter or margarine
175g/6oz caster sugar
2 eggs, beaten
1 egg yolk
1 teaspoon vanilla extract
200ml/7 fl oz low fat crème fraîche
250g/9oz blueberries, washed

For the topping
75g/3oz plain flour
50g/2oz soft brown sugar
½ teaspoon ground cinnamon
pinch salt
75g/3oz butter

Grease and line the base of a 23cm (9 inch) square cake tin.

In a bowl, mix together the flour, baking powder, bicarbonate of soda and salt. In another bowl, cream together the butter and sugar until light and fluffy. Beat in the eggs and the vanilla essence. Fold in the flour and the crème fraîche. Fold in the blueberries. Spoon the mixture into the prepared tin.

To make the topping, measure the flour, sugar, cinnamon, and salt into a bowl. Cut the butter into small cubes and rub in to make a crumble topping. Spoon this over the cake mixture.

For a two-oven Aga, place the shelf on the floor of the roasting oven, slide in the cake and then put the cold shelf two runners above. Bake for 30-35 minutes.

For a three- or four-oven Aga, hang the shelf on the bottom set of runners in the baking oven and slide in the cake. Bake for 40-45 minutes.

The cake is baked when it has shrunk from the sides of the tin and a skewer comes out clean. Cool on a wire rack and then cut into squares.

PLUM CRUNCH CAKE

In the Autumn I am frequently asked for recipes using plums - this is the one that I like the best!

225g/8oz plums
2 eggs
1 egg yolk
150g/5oz butter, softened
150g/5oz caster sugar
150g/5oz self-raising flour
1 orange, zest and juice

For the topping
1¹/₂ tablespoons lemon juice
225g/8oz caster sugar
25g/1oz sugar cubes, roughly crushed

Butter and line the base of a ¹/₂kg (1 lb) loaf tin.

Halve and stone the plums. Roughly chop half of them into chunks and cut the remaining plums into wedges.

Place the eggs, egg yolk, butter, caster sugar, flour, orange zest and 2 tablespoons of orange juice into a mixing bowl and stir well with a wooden spoon until smooth. Fold in the chopped plums and then spoon the mixture into the prepared tin. Scatter over the plum wedges.

For a two-oven Aga, stand the tin in the large roasting tin and lay over a piece of foil from back to front. Slide the roasting tin onto the bottom set of runners of the roasting oven. Put the cold shelf on the third set of runners from the bottom of the roasting oven.

For a three- or four-oven Aga, hang the shelf on the bottom set of runners in the baking oven. Slide in the loaf tin.

Bake the cake for 40-50 minutes, until a skewer inserted in the middle comes out clean. Leave the cake in the tin for 10 minutes. Turn out and stand upright on a wire rack placed over a baking tray.

Mix the remaining orange juice, lemon juice and caster sugar together. Spoon it over the warm cake and sprinkle over the crushed sugar. Cool for at least an hour before cutting.

PEACH AND STRAWBERRY TORTE

This torte makes a great pudding when warm, or a lovely summer cake to serve cold. It's easy to make and although I've used peaches and strawberries other fruits such as plums and apples are equally as good.

175g/6oz ground almonds
175g/6oz butter, softened or margarine
175g/6oz self-raising flour
175g/6oz caster sugar
1 teaspoon ground cinnamon
1 egg, beaten
1 egg yolk
3 peaches, sliced
225g/8oz strawberries, hulled and sliced
icing sugar for dusting

Grease a 23cm (9 inch) spring-release cake tin.

Place the almonds, butter, flour, caster sugar, cinnamon and eggs into a bowl and either by hand or by using a mixer, stir until smooth and evenly mixed. Be careful not to over mix.

Spread half the mixture into the base of the greased tin. Lay the prepared fruit on top. Gently spoon the remaining torte mixture over the fruit. It does not matter if you don't get even coverage and some fruit is showing through.

For a two-oven Aga, place the shelf on the floor of the roasting oven and slide in the cake tin. Put the cold shelf on the second set of runners from the bottom of the oven and bake for 50 minutes to 1 hour.

For a three- or four-oven Aga, place the oven shelf on the bottom set of runners of the baking oven. Slide in the torte and bake for 50 minutes to 1 hour.

The torte is cooked when the top is golden brown, dry looking on top and slightly shrunk from the sides of the tin.

Cool the torte for 10 minutes in the tin and then release. Dust with icing sugar.

This is delicious hot or cold.

Serves 8

RASPBERRY AND MARZIPAN ROULADE

Though this is a cake, the fresh raspberries and cream make it more of a pudding. It's easy to make in the Aga but I advise you to use Bake-O-Glide which prevents it from sticking and makes it easy to roll up.

5 eggs, separated
150g/5oz caster sugar
1 teaspoon vanilla essence
75g/3oz marzipan, cut into small cubes
3 tablespoons plain flour

For the filling
300ml/1/2 pint double cream, whipped to soft peaks
25g/1oz caster sugar
225g/8oz raspberries
icing sugar to dust

Line the large roasting tin with Bake-O-Glide.

Whisk together the egg yolks and the caster sugar until pale and thick. Fold in the vanilla essence and marzipan. Sift over the flour and fold in.

In a clean bowl, whisk the egg whites until they form stiff peaks. Fold one tablespoon of egg white into the yolk mixture, mixing well. Gently fold the remaining egg white into the yolk mixture and then pour into the prepared tin. Level off the surface.

For a two-oven Aga, hang the tin on the bottom set of runners of the roasting oven and slide in the cold shelf onto the third set of runners from the top.

For the three- or four-oven Aga, hang the tin on the third set of runners from the top of the baking oven.

Bake the roulade for 15-20 minutes, until risen, golden and firm to the touch.

Leave to stand for 5 minutes and then turn onto a plain sheet of Bake-O-Glide. Cool.

When cold, remove the lining sheet of Bake-O-Glide and spread on the whipped cream. Scatter over the raspberries and sprinkle over the caster sugar. Roll the roulade from one of the short ends and roll onto a platter. Dust with icing sugar. Serve chilled.

BANANA AND CRUNCHIE LOAF

I came across this recipe in Australia; it's a new twist on the usual banana loaf. The Crunchie bars add a chewy texture, a lovely contrast to the soft bananas. I have tried baking this loaf in the baking oven, but for best results use the roasting oven.

200g/7oz self-raising flour
¼ teaspoon bicarbonate of soda
pinch of salt
2 eggs, beaten
75g/3oz margarine
175g/6oz caster sugar
450g/1lb bananas (or 3 large), mashed
2 Crunchie bars, roughly chopped

Grease and line the base of a deep ½kg (1lb) loaf tin.

Place the flour, bicarbonate of soda, salt, eggs, margarine and sugar in a bowl and stir to mix. The mixture will be firm at this stage. Add the mashed bananas and stir in. Spoon the mixture into the prepared tin and scatter over the chopped Crunchie bars. Swirl through with a round bladed knife to incorporate the honeycomb mixture.

For a two-, three- or four-oven Aga, put the shelf on the floor of the roasting oven. Put in the loaf tin and slide the cold shelf onto the second set of runners from the top of the oven. Bake for 50 minutes to 1 hour until risen, golden brown and a skewer inserted in the middle comes out clean. Check the cake after 35-40 minutes and if it is browning too much, slide a piece of foil loosely over the top of the cake.

Cool for 5 minutes and then remove from the tin and cool on a wire rack. Slice and serve with butter, if liked.

COCONUT LOAF

I like to eat this coconut loaf both freshly baked and then the next day, thickly sliced, toasted on the simmering plate and served with a butter and ginger conserve.

2 eggs
300ml/10 fl oz milk
1 teaspoon vanilla essence
375g/13oz plain flour
2 teaspoons baking powder
2 teaspoons cinnamon
225g/8oz caster sugar
150g/5oz desiccated coconut
75g/3oz butter, melted

Grease and line the base of a 1 kg (2lb) loaf tin.

Place the eggs, milk and vanilla essence in a basin and beat together. Put the flour, baking powder, cinnamon, sugar and coconut in a bowl and stir to mix. Stir the egg mixture into the flour and when combined, stir in the melted butter. When the cake is mixed, spoon into the prepared tin.

For a two-, three- or four-oven Aga. place the shelf on the floor of the roasting oven. Put in the loaf tin and slide the cold shelf onto the second set of runners from the top of the roasting oven. Bake the loaf for 50 minutes to 1 hour, until risen, golden brown and a skewer inserted in the top comes out clean. Check the cake after 40 minutes, and if it is browning too much slide over a sheet of foil and continue baking.

Cool for 5-10 minutes in the tin and then remove and cool on a wire rack.

COCONUT AND LIME LOAF CAKE

The coconut in this loaf makes it lovely and moist while the limes give it an exotic flavour. You can substitute lemons for the limes.

110g/4oz self-raising flour
110g/4oz softened butter or margarine
110g/4oz caster sugar
25g/1oz desiccated coconut
grated rind and juice 1 lime
2 eggs, beaten

For the topping
2 tablespoons caster sugar
grated rind and juice 1 lime
1 tablespoon desiccated coconut to sprinkle on the top

Grease and line the base of a ¹/₂kg (1lb) loaf tin.

Place all the cake ingredients into a mixing bowl and stir with a wooden spoon until smooth, light and fluffy. Spoon into the prepared tin and level off the top.

For a two-oven Aga, place the shelf on the floor of the roasting oven and put in the loaf tin. Slide the cold shelf onto the second set of runners from the top of the oven. Bake for 35-40 minutes.

For a three- and four-oven Aga, put the shelf on the bottom set of runners of the baking oven. Slide in the cake and bake for 40-45 minutes. The cake will be cooked when it is golden brown, slightly shrunk from the sides of the tin and when a skewer inserted into the middle comes out clean. Cool in the tin and then turn out onto a wire rack.

For the topping, mix the lime juice and sugar together in a basin and spoon over the warm cake, allowing the liquid to soak in. Mix the coconut and lime rind together and sprinkle over the top of the cake to decorate.

CHOCOLATE AND ORANGE CAKE

Driving home one day, I was trying to think of a cake to make for one of my Aga cookery days at home. I had just been given a Terry's Chocolate Orange as a gift and it reminded me of this wonderful classic combination.

3 eggs
175g/6oz self-raising flour
175g/6oz caster sugar
175g/6oz soft margarine
grated rind 2 oranges
juice 1 orange
1 tablespoon cocoa powder, blended with 2 tablespoons hot water

For the icing
175g/6oz icing sugar
50g/2oz soft margarine
juice 1 orange

Line the base of a 23cm (9 inch) deep cake tin with a circle of Bake-O-Glide.

Place the eggs, self-raising flour, caster sugar, soft margarine, orange rind and juice in a mixing bowl. Stir until smooth with a wooden spoon. Using half the mixture, place spoonfuls of mixture at random in the base of the prepared tin.

Add the blended cocoa powder to the remaining cake mixture and stir until blended. Use this mixture to fill in the gaps in the cake tin. Swirl the two mixtures together using a round-bladed knife to achieve a marbled effect.

For a two-oven Aga, place the shelf on the floor of the roasting oven, slide in the cake tin and then slide the cold shelf onto the second set of runners from the bottom of the oven.

Bake for 20-25 minutes, until risen and firm to touch in the middle of the cake.

For a three- or four-oven Aga, hang the shelf on the second set of runners from the bottom of the baking oven and slide in the cake tin. Bake the cake for 25-30 minutes, until risen and firm to the touch in the middle of the cake.

Cool the cake for 5 minutes in the tin, then remove and cool on a rack.

Prepare the icing; sieve the icing sugar into a mixing bowl, add the margarine and the orange juice. Beat well to make a smooth icing. Spread over the top of the cake.

CHOCOLATE AND ORANGE BISCUIT CAKE

This is a slightly more grown-up version of the Chocolate biscuit cake my children used to make at school. Using Duchy Originals Orange Biscuits makes this cake special. Though you don't actually bake this biscuit cake in the Aga it's such a good recipe that I couldn't resist including it in the book.

200g/7oz plain, dark chocolate
125g/5oz butter
1 tablespoon honey
250g/8oz orange flavoured biscuits
50g/2oz rice pops

Place the chocolate, butter and honey into a mixing bowl and stand on the back of the Aga until the chocolate and butter have melted. Stir well.

Place the biscuits in a plastic bag and crush roughly but not to a fine powder. Tip the biscuits and the rice pops into the chocolate mixture. Stir to coat well.

Line the small roasting tin with Bake-O-Glide. Spread the biscuit mixture in the tin. Press down well and level off.

Chill well until set. Cut into fingers before serving.

DOUBLE CHOCOLATE BISCOTTI

Biscotti are wonderful, dry Italian biscuits great for dipping in your coffee or a glass of the Italian dessert wine, Vin Santo. They keep very well in an air-tight tin.

110g/4oz butter
110g/4oz plain chocolate
50g/2oz cocoa powder
200g/7oz plain flour
1½ teaspoons baking powder
½ teaspoon salt
225g/8oz caster sugar
2 eggs, beaten
1 teaspoon vanilla essence
110g/4oz chopped pistachios, optional

Place the butter and the chocolate in a basin and stand at the back of the Aga until melted.

Mix together the cocoa, flour, baking powder, salt and sugar in a mixing bowl.

Stir the melted butter and chocolate into the dry ingredients. Add the beaten eggs followed by the chopped nuts if using, and the vanilla essence.

Line the large Aga baking tray with a sheet of Bake-O-Glide. Spoon the biscotti dough onto the baking tray and shape into a rough, oblong shape.

For the two-oven Aga, hang the tin on the bottom set of runners of the roasting oven. Slide the cold shelf onto the second set of runners from the top of the oven. Bake for 20 minutes.

For the three- or four-oven Aga, hang the tin on the second set of runners from the bottom of the baking oven and bake for 20-25 minutes. The biscotti will have finished their first baking when they are firm to the touch and dry on the top.

Cool the biscotti in the tin for 10 minutes and then cool further on a cooling rack. Place on a chopping board and cut the biscotti into slices about 2cm ($^3/_4$ inch) thick. Lay the slices on the baking tray and return to the oven, as above, for 10 minutes, to dry out.

Cool on a wire rack.

WALNUT AND CRANBERRY BISCOTTI

Walnuts and cranberries help make these biscotti ideal Christmas gifts.

175g/6oz walnuts, roughly chopped
1 teaspoon baking powder
300g/10oz plain flour
300g/10oz caster sugar
¹/₂ teaspoon salt
4 eggs
1 teaspoon vanilla essence
75g/3oz dried cranberries

Measure the walnuts, baking powder, flour, sugar and salt into a large mixing bowl. In a separate bowl beat together the eggs and the vanilla essence and add these to the dry ingredients. Mix well and then stir in the cranberries.

Line a large baking tray with a sheet of Bake-O-Glide. Tip the mixture onto the middle of the lined tray and spread out to a rough oblong shape.

For a two-oven Aga, hang the tin on the bottom set of runners of the roasting oven and slide in the cold shelf on the second set of runners from the top. Bake the biscotti for 20 minutes, until dry on the top and just colouring to a golden brown.

For a three- or four-oven Aga, hang the tray on the second set of runners from the bottom of the baking oven and bake for 20-25 minutes, until dry on the top and just colouring to a golden brown.

Cool the biscotti in the tin for 10 minutes and then transfer to a cooling rack. When cold, place the biscotti on a board and cut into 2cm (³/₄ inch) width slices. Return the slices to the baking tray and then place the tray in the oven again, this time for a further 10 minutes for the biscotti to dry out. Cool on a wire rack.

CHOCOLATE BROWNIES

Chocolate Brownies are very popular, but can often be too rich or too dry. I have worked on this recipe a lot, much to the delight of my children and their friends. I sometimes replace the walnuts with chocolate chunks or chips, depending upon who is home. This is the one recipe in this book that I feel is best cooked in the baking oven; the slightly longer cooking time helps produce a more moist cake. Having said that, the brownies made in the roasting oven are still very good.

200g/7oz butter or margarine
450g/1lb caster sugar
4 level tablespoons cocoa powder
175g/6oz plain flour
pinch salt
4 eggs, beaten
2 teaspoons vanilla extract
100g/3¹/₂oz chopped walnuts

Line the small roasting tin with a sheet of Bake-O-Glide.

Place the butter in a basin and stand at the back of the Aga until the butter has melted.

Measure the sugar, cocoa powder, plain flour and salt into a mixing bowl. Stir well. Pour in the melted butter, stir lightly and then add the beaten eggs and vanilla extract. Stir until all the dry ingredients are mixed in, but be careful not to beat in too much air. The brownies need to have a firm, slightly sticky finish under the sugary crust. Fold in the chopped walnuts. Pour the mixture into the prepared tin.

For a two-oven Aga, hang the tin on the bottom set of runners of the roasting oven and slide the cold tray in two runners above. Bake for 25-30 minutes.

For a three- or four-oven Aga, hang the tin on the bottom set of runners of the baking oven and bake for 40-45 minutes.

When cooked the brownie should be firm on the top and a skewer should come out clean.

Cool the brownies in the tin and cut into squares.

CHOCOLATE CHIP COOKIE BARS

These bars are like a kind of thick chocolate chip cookie. The ingredients may seem rich but you can always cut the finished cookie bars down in size. Beware they are very moorish!

225g/8oz butter or margarine
300g/10oz soft brown sugar
1 teaspoon vanilla extract
2 eggs, beaten
175g/6oz plain flour
200g/7oz porridge oats
pinch salt
1/2 teaspoon baking powder
200g/7oz chocolate chips

Line the small roasting tin with Bake-O-Glide.

Place the butter and sugar in a mixing bowl and beat together until light and fluffy. Beat in the eggs and the vanilla essence, adding a little flour after the addition of each egg. Fold in the remaining flour, porridge oats, baking powder and chocolate chips.

Spoon the dough into the prepared tin and smooth the top.

For a two-oven Aga, hang the tin on the bottom set of runners of the roasting oven and slide the cold shelf two runners above. Bake for about 35 minutes.

For a three- or four-oven Aga, hang the tin on the second set of runners from the top of the baking oven and bake for 40-45 minutes.

Bake until dry on the top and firm to the touch in the middle. Cool in the tin. When cold remove from the tin, peel off the Bake-O-Glide and cut into bars.

Makes about 24

CHOCOLATE AND ORANGE MUFFINS

These muffins are seriously rich and 'wicked' to eat. Unlike most muffins these will keep for a day or two, if there are any left over!

110g/4oz butter, softened
110g/4oz caster sugar
1 egg, beaten
142ml carton soured cream
a little milk, if needed
150g/5oz plain flour
1/2 teaspoon bicarbonate of soda
1/2 teaspoon baking powder
pinch of salt
110g/4oz milk chocolate, chopped or chocolate chunks
zest of 1 orange

Line a muffin tin with 12 paper cases.

Cream the butter and sugar until pale and fluffy. Beat in the egg lightly and then add half the soured cream. Mix to combine. Stir in the flour, bicarbonate of soda and the baking powder. Stir in the remaining soured cream and a little milk, if needed, to make a soft dropping consistency. Gently fold in the chocolate and the zest of the orange. Take care not to over-mix. Spoon into the muffin tins.

Hang the shelf on the third set of runners from the top of the roasting oven. Slide in the muffin tin and bake for 25-30 minutes until risen and firm when given a gentle squeeze.

Best served warm.

Makes 12 muffins

CHERRY SHORTBREAD

A variation on a standard shortbread, the cherries add sweetness and colour. As with all shortbreads, you really should use butter to make this.

175g/6oz plain flour
110g/4oz butter, at room temperature
50g/2oz caster sugar
25g/1oz glacé cherries, halved

Line a 23cm (9 inch) square tin. There is no need to butter the sides. Place the flour, butter and caster sugar in a mixing bowl and rub in the butter to resemble breadcrumbs. Stir in the cherries and then lightly work the mixture to a dough consistency.

Press the dough into the prepared tin and smooth off the top. Crimp the edges if liked and prick the top with a fork.

To bake the shortbread in a two-oven Aga, put the shelf on the floor of the roasting oven. Put in the shortbread and slide the cold shelf onto the second set of runners from the bottom of the oven. Bake for 20 minutes until dry and a pale golden colour.

For a three- or four-oven Aga, put the shelf on the bottom set of runners of the baking oven and bake the shortbread for 20-25 minutes until dry and a pale golden colour.

Mark the shortbread into squares while still warm. Cool in the tin.

CARAMEL FINGERS

This is a highly calorific cake often referred to as 'Millionaire's Shortbread'. Keep refrigerated to ensure the filling holds firm.

225g/8oz butter
110g/4oz caster sugar
350g/12oz self-raising flour

For the filling
1 x 397g can condensed milk
175g/6 oz butter or margarine
225g/8 oz caster sugar
4 tablespoons golden syrup

For the topping
350g/12oz plain or milk chocolate, melted
(use lower cocoa content chocolate as it doesn't set
as hard and the fingers are then easier to cut and eat)

Line the small roasting tin with a sheet of Bake-O-Glide.

To make the shortbread base, place the butter, sugar and flour into a mixing bowl and rub in the butter. Continue to work the dough until the butter softens and mixes with the dry ingredients. Press the dough into the base of the lined tin. Level the top.

For the two-oven Aga, hang the shelf on the bottom set of runners of the roasting oven and slide the cold shelf onto the second set of runners from the bottom. Bake for 20-30 minutes until looking dry and a very pale golden.

For a three- oven or four-oven Aga, hang the tin on the bottom set of runners of the baking oven and bake the shortbread for 25-30 minutes, until looking dry and a pale golden.

Cool in the tin.

Use a heavy-based saucepan to prepare the filling. I know that some people boil the un-opened cans of condensed milk to make the filling but I don't think it particularly safe, and simmering the can in the oven in a pan of water has usually proved unsatisfactory. So, put all the ingredients in a heavy-based, roomy saucepan. Place on the simmering plate and heat until the butter has melted and the mixture has begun to gently bubble. Continue stirring for about 5 minutes until thick. Spread over the shortbread and leave to cool until set firm.

When the caramel is cold, pour over the melted chocolate and spread and swirl evenly. Cool.

Remove the caramel shortbread from the tin and peel off the Bake-O-Glide. Place the shortbread on a chopping board. Heat a large, sharp knife with hot water and dry immediately. Use this to cut the caramel shortbread into fingers or squares.

LITTLE ALMOND CAKES

These not so little almond cakes are moist and delicious. They are easy to make and don't need any decorating.

150g/5½oz softened butter or margarine
200g/7oz caster sugar
4 eggs
110g/4oz ground almonds
60g/2oz plain flour
½ teaspoon almond essence

Line a 12 hole muffin tin with paper cases.

Place the butter and the caster sugar in a basin and mix well until creamed and fluffy. Beat in the eggs one at a time, alternating with the flour. Fold in any remaining flour and the ground almonds and finally the almond essence. Spoon the mixture into the prepared muffin tins.

Hang the oven shelf on the bottom set of runners of the roasting oven. Slide in the muffin tin and bake the almond cakes for 12-15 minutes, until risen, golden brown and firm to the touch.

Cool on a rack and dust with caster sugar.

Makes 12 cakes

ECCLES CAKES

These are a great favourite in my family. My mother, whose pastry was the best I have ever eaten, made these from scratch. I am not a good pastry maker, so I use ready-rolled puff pastry.

375g packet ready-rolled puff pastry
25g/1oz butter, melted
110g/4oz currants
50g/2oz caster sugar
¹/₂ teaspoon ground mixed spice

For the glaze
1 egg white
caster sugar

Mix together the butter, currants, sugar and mixed spice.

Unroll the pastry and stamp out an even number of circles using a 9cm (3¹/₂ inch) cutter.

Lay half the rounds on a baking tray and top these with the filling, leaving a small border to seal the cakes. Lay a pastry round on top of the filling and lightly seal. Cut three slashes in the top of the Eccles cakes. Brush the tops with lightly beaten egg white and dust with caster sugar.

Hang the tin on the third set of runners of the roasting oven and bake the Eccles cakes for 15-20 minutes, until risen and a very pale golden brown. Best eaten slightly warm.

CHOCOLATE ECLAIRS

This recipe is from my book *The Traditional Aga Cookery Book*, but as it's so useful I have included it here. The eclair mixture is cooked in rounds and shaped with a spoon instead of a piping bag and can be filled with cooked apple and cream.

For the Choux pastry
2¹/₂oz/65g plain flour
pinch salt
150ml¹/₄pint water
2oz/50g butter-cubed
2 eggs, well beaten

For the filling
300ml/¹/₂pint double cream

For the chocolate glacé icing
75g/3oz plain chocolate
1oz/25g butter
3 tablespoons warm water
¹/₂ teaspoon vanilla essence
175g/6oz icing sugar

Sieve the flour and salt. Put the water and butter into a saucepan and stand on the simmering plate and heat to melt the butter. Then bring to a brisk boil and remove from the heat. Quickly tip in all the flour and beat well with a wooden spoon. Return to the heat and stir briskly until the dough forms a ball and the sides of the pan are left clean. Remove from the heat.

Add the eggs gradually, beating between each addition. I find a hand-held electric mixer best. Beat until a smooth, shiny mixture is formed.

Fit a piping bag with a 1cm (¹/₂inch) plain nozzle and fill it with the pastry. Pipe lengths 10cm (4 inch) long onto a greased baking tray.

Place the shelf on the lowest set of runners of the roasting oven and bake for 20-25 minutes until risen and golden brown. Remove from the oven and slit the sides to allow steam to escape. Return to the oven for 5 minutes to dry out. Cool on a wire rack.

Whip the cream and fill the éclairs. Cover the tops with the icing and leave to set.

To make the icing, break the chocolate into a basin, add the butter and stand the basin on top of the Aga to melt. When melted, add the water and vanilla essence. Gradually add the icing sugar, beating until smooth. Coat the éclairs. For a pudding, fill the éclairs with cream, pile high on a dish and pour the chocolate icing over them.

For a coffee glacé icing variation
2 teaspoons instant coffee granules
2 tablespoons hot water
225g/8oz icing sugar

Mix the coffee granules and hot water until dissolved. Sieve the sugar in a bowl, gradually add the coffee and beat well until the icing is thick enough to coat the back of a wooden spoon.

SCONES

Scones are so easy to make and yet how often do you see and sample thin and bitter tasting ones? This is a basic recipe for plain scones but you can add a handful of sultanas, chopped apple, and grated cheese for variety.

225g/8oz self-raising flour
25g/1oz butter
pinch salt
25g/1oz caster sugar
150ml-200ml/5-7fl oz milk

Put the flour and salt in a mixing bowl and add the butter. Rub the butter into the flour until the mixture resembles fine breadcrumbs. Stir in the sugar. Add 150ml (5fl oz) of the milk and stir into the flour using a table knife. Mix just enough to make a firm, but sticky dough. Add more milk if needed.

Turn the dough onto a lightly floured worktop and press out to the thickness of your hand. Do not use a rolling pin as you will be tempted to make biscuits and not scones. Stamp out scone shapes using a sharp cutter and place the scones on a baking tray. Brush the tops with a little milk.

Hang the tin on the third set of runners from the top of the roasting oven and bake for 12-15 minutes, until risen, golden brown and just firm when squeezed round the middle. Cool on a wire rack.

Serve with butter or cream and jam.

RICH FRUIT CAKE

This is a standard fruit cake recipe traditionally used as a celebration cake.

450g/1lb plain flour
1/2 level teaspoon salt
1 level teaspoon ground cinnamon
1 level teaspoon ground mixed spice
450g/1lb sultanas
350g/12oz raisins
350g/12oz currants
225g/8oz glacé cherries, halved and washed
50g/2oz walnuts, chopped
300g/10¹/₂ oz butter, softened
300g/10¹/₂ oz soft brown sugar
5 eggs, beaten
2 tablespoons black treacle
finely grated rind 1 lemon
4 tablespoons brandy

Grease and line a 23cm (9 inch) deep, round cake tin or a 20cm (8 inch) deep, square cake tin.

Mix the flour and spices together in a bowl. Pick over the dried fruit and mix together in a bowl adding the cherries and the nuts.

Place the butter and sugar into a large mixing bowl and cream until light and fluffy. Beat in the eggs, a little at a time, adding 1 tablespoon flour with each addition. Fold in the remaining flour followed by the fruit. When mixed well, add the treacle, lemon rind and the brandy. Mix well but gently. Spoon into the prepared tin and level the top.

Put the shelf on the floor of the simmering oven and put in the cake. Bake until an even brown on the top, slightly shrunk from the sides of the tin and a skewer inserted in the middle comes out clean. This can take anything from 6 to 18 hours! I leave mine for 12 hours, usually overnight. (Remember to leave yourself a note on the breakfast table!) Because the cooking time is so variable, I suggest that if you are new to your Aga, you bake the cake during the day and monitor the amount of time it needs. Then make a note on the recipe for future reference.

Cool in the tin.

JEAN'S MOIST FRUIT CAKE

Jean is my neighbour, who is a very good cook, and we often discuss ideas for baking. This recipe that she gave me is now one of my favourites. It's so easy to make, is delicious and keeps well.

250g/9oz sultanas
250g/9oz raisins
225g/8oz soft brown sugar
1/2 teaspoon cinnamon
1/2 teaspoon ground ginger
175g/6oz butter
250ml/8 fl oz water
3 eggs, beaten
150g/5oz plain flour
150g/5oz self-raising flour
1/2 teaspoon bicarbonate of soda
175g/6oz glacé cherries, washed and chopped

Grease and line the base of a 20cm (8 inch) deep, round cake tin.

If you are using the Cake Baker, place the oven shelf on the floor of the roasting oven and stand in the empty Cake Baker to heat through while making the cake.

Put the raisins, sultanas, sugar, spices, butter and water into a saucepan. Place on the simmering plate and stir until the butter has melted and the sugar dissolved. Continue to stir while bringing to the boil. Simmer for 3-4 minutes and then remove from the heat. Cool.

In a bowl, mix together the flours and the bicarbonate of soda. Stir in the cherries.

Returning to the saucepan, stir in the eggs into the fruit mixture and then pour this mixture into the flours. Fold in well and then spoon the mixture into the prepared tin.

If using the Cake Baker, stand the tin in the trivet, remove the Cake Baker from the oven, place in the cake, re-cover and return to the oven for 1-1$^1/_2$ hours.

For a two-oven Aga, stand the cake tin in the large roasting tin. Cover loosely with foil from back to front. Slide the tin onto the bottom set of runners of the roasting tin. Put the cold shelf on the second set of runners from the top of the oven and bake the cake for 55 minutes to 1 hour.

For a three- or four-oven Aga, place the oven shelf on the bottom set of runners of the baking oven, slide in the cake and bake for 1-1$^1/_4$ hours.

The cake, when baked, will be risen, firm to touch, slightly shrunk from the side of the tin and a skewer will come out clean. Cool in the tin for 15 minutes and then turn onto a wire rack to cool further.

RICH CHRISTMAS CAKE

Make this cake at the beginning of Advent and then each week before Christmas pour on a little brandy to make a delicious cake.

450g/1lb currants
225g/8oz sultanas
225g/8oz raisins
110g/4oz candied peel, chopped
175g/6oz glacé cherries, halved and washed
300g/10oz plain flour
pinch salt
1/2 teaspoon mixed spice
1/2 teaspoon cinnamon
300g/10oz butter
300g/10oz soft brown sugar
grated rind 1/2 lemon
6 eggs, beaten
75g/3oz ground almonds
3 tablespoons brandy
1 tablespoon black treacle
2 tablespoons milk

Grease and line the base of a 23cm (9 inch) deep, round cake tin.

Place all the fruit in a mixing bowl and add the flour and spices. Stir round to coat the fruit in the flour.

Cream together the butter and sugar until pale and fluffy. Beat in the eggs, adding a little of the almonds between each addition of egg. Stir in the fruit mixture and then add the brandy, treacle and milk. Stir to mix all the ingredients well but do not over-mix.

Spoon the mixture into the prepared tin and level the surface.

For a two- and three-oven Aga, put the oven shelf on the floor of the simmering oven (there is no need to use a shelf for the four-oven Aga, just put the cake directly on the floor of the oven). Put the cake into the simmering oven and bake for 10-12 hours or overnight, until the cake is dry on the top, shrunk from the side of the tin and a skewer inserted in the middle comes out clean. Cool in the tin.

When cold, wrap in foil and store in a cool place. Each week until decorating the cake, prick the top with a skewer and spoon over 3 tablespoons brandy.

DUNDEE CAKE

A Dundee cake is a light fruit cake that keeps well for several weeks in a tin.

225g/8oz butter
225g/8oz caster sugar
grated rind 1 lemon
4 eggs, beaten
225g/8oz plain flour
50g/2oz ground almonds
175g/6oz sultanas
175g/6oz currants
50g/2oz raisins
50g/2oz candied peel, chopped
1 tablespoon sherry
1 tablespoon milk
50g/2oz blanched almonds to top

Grease and line the base of a 20.5cm (8 inch) deep, round cake tin with Bake-O-Glide.

Place the butter and sugar in a mixing bowl and beat together until light and fluffy. Beat in the lemon rind and then the eggs, a little at a time. Mix a teaspoon of flour between each addition of egg. Fold in the fruits and finally the sherry, taking care not to over mix. Spoon the mixture into the prepared tin.

Brush the top with milk (this will stop the nuts from sinking) and place the almonds on the top.

For a two-oven Aga, place the shelf on the floor of the roasting oven, put in the cake and slide the cold shelf on the second set of runners from the top. Bake the cake for 30 minutes and then move the cake to the simmering oven. Continue baking for 2-2½ hours, until golden brown and a skewer inserted in the middle of the cake comes out clean. Cool in the tin.

For a three- or four-oven Aga, place the shelf on the floor of the baking oven. Put in the cake and bake for 1³/₄-2 hours until the cake is golden brown and a skewer inserted in the middle comes out clean. Cool in the tin.

GLACE FRUIT CAKE

Instead of the traditional marzipan and icing, this cake is decorated with a variety of glacé fruits set off with a pretty seasonal ribbon.

110g/4oz glacé cherries, halved and rinsed
50g/2oz dried apricots, chopped
225g/8oz currants
225g/8oz sultanas
225g/8oz raisins
50g/2oz candied peel, chopped
grated rind 1 lemon
100ml/4fl oz brandy
50g/2oz blanched almonds, chopped
50g/2oz Brazil nuts, chopped
225g/8oz butter
225g/8oz soft brown sugar
4 eggs, beaten
225g/8oz plain flour
2 teaspoons mixed spice

To decorate
4 tablespoon apricot jam
glacé fruits

Grease and line the base of a 20.5 cm (8 inch) deep, round cake tin.

Place the apricots, currants, sultanas, raisins, candied peel, lemon rind and brandy in a bowl and leave to steep for several hours or overnight. Add the nuts.

Cream the butter and the sugar together until light and fluffy. Beat in the eggs a little at a time. Add a little flour with each addition of egg. Fold in the remaining flour and the mixed spice. Add the soaked fruit and the nuts and stir in. Spoon the mixture into the prepared tin and level the top.

Place the oven shelf on the floor of the simmering oven of a two or three-oven Aga (there is no need to use a shelf for the four-oven Aga, just put the cake directly on the floor of the oven). Bake for 12-14 hours or overnight.

When the cake is cooked it will look dry on the top, have shrunk from the sides of the tin and a skewer inserted in the middle will come out clean. Cool in the tin.

To decorate the cake, brush the top generously with the apricot jam and arrange a selection of glacé fruits on the top. Tie a decorative ribbon round the cake.

GOLDEN FRUIT CAKE

This cake is a lovely golden colour when cut, with a flavour that suggests just a hint of saffron. It can be stored and then decorated as a Christmas or celebration cake.

110g/4oz dried apricots, chopped
225g/8oz sultanas
3 tablespoons rum
pinch saffron strands
110g/4oz almonds, chopped
200g/7oz glacé cherries, rinsed and chopped
110g/4oz tropical medley dried fruits, roughly copped
150g/5oz candied peel, chopped
grated rind 2 oranges
225g/8oz butter, softened
225g/8oz caster sugar
4 eggs, beaten
225g/8oz plain flour
pinch salt
50g/2oz ground almonds
1 teaspoon ground ginger

Grease and line the base of a 20.5cm (8 inch) deep, round cake tin.

Put the apricots, sultanas, rum and saffron in a bowl, stir well and leave to soak for several hours or overnight. Add the almonds, cherries, tropical fruits, candied peel and the rind of the oranges.

Place the butter and sugar in a bowl and cream until light and fluffy. Gradually add the eggs, adding a little flour after each addition. Fold in the remaining flour, salt, mixed spice and the ginger. Gently stir in the fruit and nut mixture. Spoon the mixture into the prepared tin and level the top.

For the two- and three-oven Aga put the shelf on the floor of the simmering oven (there is no need to use a shelf for the four-oven Aga, just put the cake directly on the floor of the oven). Put the cake in the oven and bake for 10-14 hours until the cake has slightly shrunk from the sides of the tin and a skewer inserted in the middle comes out cleanly. Cool in the tin.

WELSH AFTERNOON FRUIT AND CHEESE CAKE

In Yorkshire, it's traditional to eat a piece of Wensleydale cheese with a slice of fruit cake. My variation on this tradition has a Welsh twist, combining within the cake mild Caerphilly cheese with apricots, sultanas, raisins and apples.

250g/8oz plain flour
1 teaspoon baking powder
pinch salt
250g/8oz Welsh butter, softened
250g/8oz soft brown sugar
4 eggs, beaten
1 teaspoon vanilla essence
2 teaspoons ground mixed spice
grated zest 1 lemon
110g/4oz dried apricots, chopped
75g/3oz sultanas
50g/2oz raisins
2 eating apples, peeled, quartered and grated
125g/5oz Caerphilly cheese, cut into small cubes
1 tablespoon Demerara sugar

Butter and line the base of a 23cm (8 inch) deep cake tin.

If you are using the Cake Baker put this in the roasting oven to pre-heat whilst making the cake.

Mix together the flour, baking powder and salt.

In a separate bowl, cream together the butter and sugar until light and fluffy. Beat in the eggs and the vanilla essence, adding a little flour with each addition. Fold in the remaining flour. Mix together the mixed spice, lemon rind, apricots, sultanas, raisins, grated apple and the cheese. Stir gently into the cake mixture.

Spoon the mixture into the prepared cake tin. Sprinkle over the Demerara sugar.

If using the Cake Baker, place the cake in the trivet and put it into the hot Cake Baker. Return the Cake Baker to the oven and bake for 50 minutes to 1 hour until golden brown and a skewer inserted in the middle comes out clean.

For a two-oven Aga, place the cake in the large roasting tin and cover with a sheet of foil. Slide the tin onto the bottom set of runners of the roasting oven. Slide the cold shelf onto the third set of runners from the top of the roasting oven. Bake for 55-60 minutes until the cake is golden brown and a skewer comes out clean. Cool in the tin for 10 minutes and then turn out to cool on a wire rack.

For a three- or four-oven Aga, hang the shelf on the bottom set of runners of the baking oven, slide in the cake and bake for 55-60 minutes, until the cake is golden brown and a skewer comes out clean.

Cool in the tin for 10 minutes and then remove from the tin and cool on a wire rack.

CAKES

INDEX

O

P

R

S

T

ACKNOWLEDGEMENTS

I would like to thank all of the customers and staff in the Aga shops who have kindly asked for this book. Baking is becoming popular once more and demonstrations that include baking are beginning to reflect this. As well as using my tried and tested recipes from those cookery demonstrations, I have had lots of ideas from friends and family for new recipes. I must thank, yet again, my family who have at times put up with a surfeit of bread and cakes during the testing process. It may sound blissful, but not all tests work and comments and changes are all part of the process! I have had help with equipment from Falcon Products (Bake-O-Glide), ICTC (Bakeware), Aga Cookware(Baking trays) and flour information from Shipton Mill. There is no doubt that using good quality ingredients and equipment helps to make a better end product. This is also an opportunity to thank Caroline Nisbett, who has always provided my books with such striking covers and lovely illustrations, and Jon Croft, my publisher, and his team, for their continued faith in my books!

FOR FURTHER INFORMATION

Falcon Products Ltd
Falcon House
Commerce House
Carrs Industrial Estate
Haslingden BB4 5JT

Shipton Mill Ltd
Long Newnto
Tetbury
Glocestershire GL8 8RP

ICTC
3 Caley Close
Sweet Briar Road
Norwich NR3 2BU

COOK'S NOTES

COOK'S NOTES

COOK'S NOTES

COOK'S NOTES

COOK'S NOTES

COOK'S NOTES

COOK'S NOTES

COOK'S NOTES

Aga and Rayburn Titles
by Louise Walker